WEST BROMWI
TOWN HALL

LABOR OMNIA VINCIT

This book is dedicated to the past,
present and future generations
of West Bromwich

WEST BROMWICH TOWN HALL

Anne Wilkins

West Bromwich
Library User Group

Published 2003 by
West Bromwich Library User Group.

ISBN: 0-9544367-0-9

A Cataloguing in Publication Record
for this title is available from the British Library.

Typeset in Plantin
Book design by History Into Print,
Studley, Warwickshire, B80 7LG
Printed in Great Britain

CONTENTS

ACKNOWLEDGEMENTS

It is with a sense of gratitude and sincere appreciation that I acknowledge the contribution made by John M Day, former Town Clerk, who provided so much information regarding the civic events and history of the building; Sam Chiles, who worked in the Borough Treasurer's Office from the tender age of sixteen until his retirement and supplied many details of his time in that department; Reg Thompson, who worked for the 'Corporation', and allowed us to take a peep behind the scenes on a variety of social events in the Town Hall.

Thanks are due to the many people who responded to a request for information and gave their time to assist me, purely through their interest and enthusiasm in a particular area of research, although they had never visited West Bromwich.

I would like to thank the following people who made a valuable contribution to this book, even though they may have travelled far from their native town.

List of Contributors: (in alphabetical order)

Anon of West Bromwich Chrysanthemum Society; Jean Baggott; Andrew Biggs; John Brimble; Audrey and Frank Burton; Joshua Churchman, West Bromwich Mayor 1966-1967; Margaret Dallow; Dr Gerald Gibbs; Pauline Hale; James Hayes; George Shephard Johns; Leslie Lofthouse; Dianne Mannering; Professor Elizabeth McGrath, Warburg Institute, London; Professor George Noszlopy, University of Central England; Marie Parkes; Doreen and James Shakespeare; Stanley Shakespeare; Kenneth Sower; George Spencer; George Taylor; Jill Taylor; Councillor Linda Turton; Heather Upton; Edna and Ivan Walker; Frances Walton; Gladys Welsh; Paul Wise; Doreen Young.

Royal Naval Association, London: especially Captain R McQueen and RNA members George Vernon; Bob Bolter; John Fairclough; Stan Bromilow; Douglas Newell; Donald Baker.

Royal Naval Association, West Bromwich Branch: Committee and members Derek Holden and Arthur Wright.

Sandwell Metropolitan Borough Council (SMBC): Corporate Property, Legal, Leisure Direct, and Planning staff; Mayor's Secretary; West Bromwich Town Hall Curators and staff.

Libraries: Sandwell Central Library staff, especially Robin Pearson, Central Library Manager; Maureen McCrorie; Robert Hazel; Sandwell Central Reference Library staff; Community History Archives Service (CHAS), Sandwell; Birmingham Reference Library, Local Studies Department and Music Department; County Archive Research Network, Birmingham; Middlesborough Reference Library; William Salt Library, Stafford.

Museums: Birmingham Museum and Art Gallery; Victoria and Albert Museum, London; Ironbridge Gorge Museum Trust, Shropshire; Gladstone Pottery Museum, Stoke-on-Trent; Imperial War Museum, London; Broadfield House Glass Museum, Kingswinford; Wednesbury Museum and Art Gallery.

Other Organizations and individuals:

The College of Arms, London; English Heritage Listed Buildings; Royal Horticultural Society, Wisley, Surrey; West Bromwich Local History Society, especially Brian and Moreen Wilkes; Tipton Community Heritage Centre; BBC Radio WM, Carl Chinn Programme; Guest Organist, Nigel Ogden; *Express and Star; The Black Country Bugle;* Lyng Primary School Archives, Headteacher: Malcolm Chesney; Sandwell Youth Music, Musical Directors and staff; Jubilee Arts: Trevor Pitt and staff.

Photographs: Tony Usherwood (for Sidney Darby Copyright permission); Paul McIntosh; Ronald Payne; Paul Wise; Community Archives and History Service (CHAS), Sandwell.

I wish to thank Doreen Barnfield and Brian Hopwood for their assistance with proof reading and David Froggatt for patiently retrieving many 'lost' files on my computer. I owe a vote of thanks to all members of the West Bromwich Library User Group for their loyalty and support during the last two years, especially Keith Kilvert, Derrick de Faye, and James and Doreen Shakespeare. My special thanks to Robin Pearson for editing this book and to our Treasurer, Fred Barnfield, for his encouragement during the final stages of publishing.

I would like to thank my family, especially my daughters Sue, Ruth and Pam, for their unconditional support and encouragement on this special project, although at times they must have thought that I had hibernated during the summer months when it became necessary for me to spend time collating all the research material.

I offer my sincere apologies, if by any chance, I have inadvertently omitted to mention anyone by name who has contacted me and helped with this research.

Finally, the West Bromwich Library User Group Committee wish to thank John Allen, Chairman of Sandwell Arts, for his contribution of standing as an independent referee in our application for a Lottery Grant. The 'User Group' wish to thank and express their sincere gratitude to the National Lottery's *Awards for All* Committee for their generous Queen's Award Grant to celebrate the Queen's Golden Jubilee, 2002.

Anne Wilkins (August 2002)

The West Bromwich Library User Group wish to acknowledge their appreciation of Sandwell Metropolitan Borough Council (SMBC) for their kind permission to publish the West Bromwich Coat of Arms and all images within the Town Hall. Unless otherwise stated, all photographs and programmes are reproduced with the kind permission of SMBC.

LIST OF ILLUSTRATIONS

LIST OF COLOUR PLATES

INTRODUCTION

It was during August 2000 that my interest was aroused in the history of West Bromwich Town Hall. I distinctly remember the occasion, for I read that a Banquet had been planned to celebrate the opening of the Town Hall in 1875.

I thought about that colourful and auspicious event when the rich and influential families of the town gathered for this important social occasion. I tried to visualise the colours, textures and style of the ladies gowns of that Victorian era. There must have been a tremendous air of excitement and anticipation as the guests arrived in their carriages and the ladies were escorted up the broad stairway to the gallery where they observed the scene below in the main hall.

If only the walls could talk what a wealth of stories they would tell about the life and times enacted within its portals. Then I realised that this could be achieved if members of our present community could be persuaded to write down their reminiscences of events and leisure pursuits within the building.

Past and present inhabitants of the town took up the challenge and this book is the result of their contributions. People were keen to discuss not only social events held in the Town Hall but also their memories of particular parts of the building which touched on their working and social life. So, in an attempt to answer their questions, the research widened to include the building and its contents.

This started a very interesting trail of discovery in researching the part that the Town Hall played in the public and social life of the borough. Reminiscences were collected dating from 1927 to the present day and they revealed an interesting, stimulating and amusing life within the building that equals any event enacted there in the past.

Anne Wilkins

August 2002

West Bromwich Town Hall, main entrance.

CHAPTER 1

IN THE BEGINNING

In the beginning there was the land, owned by the rich Izon family but previously part of the West Bromwich Heath before the 1804 Enclosure Act. This prime land, known as the Lodge Estate, was purchased from Messrs John York and others acting as Trustees of William Izon deceased, 'for the erection of a complex of public buildings including a town hall designed to provide accommodation for the civic business of the town; to enhance the prestige of its dignitaries and also improve the social life of the town's population in general.'

The need for new buildings was recorded by F W Hackwood the noted Black Country historian, in his book *A History of West Bromwich*:

> 'By this date (1854) there were in existence some churches and chapels; but these were the only class of public buildings to be found within the confines of the parish … (there was) an absence of public buildings for conducting the Municipal and social life of the community.'

The West Bromwich Town Improvement Commissioners between 1854 and 1882 were elected to govern and as such were responsible for the design, planning and erection of these public buildings. It would appear that some members of the community were not impressed with the proposed waste of public money on these projects and voiced their objections to the scheme in no uncertain manner. At a much later date, 1875, when these projects were a *fait accompli*, these inhabitants of the town met with some scathing comments in the *West Bromwich Weekly News*.

> 'When the question of erecting public buildings was first mooted it met, like many other good movements, with some opposition, but the antagonism of the stingy, short-sighted party has to give way before the sensible dictates of the majority who will come to recognise that there is such a wholesome doctrine as municipal respect and decency.'

The views and wishes of the majority of West Bromwich citizens won the day and the Improvement Commissioners decided to advertise a competition for architects to submit designs for these public buildings which included a town hall.
The Building News, 27 October 1871 states that:

'Twenty-nine architects submitted plans for the buildings for the consideration of the Improvement Commissioners.'

In their wisdom, and due to their lack of knowledge in architectural matters, the Town Improvement Commissioners appointed an eminent London architect, Ewan Christian ,who worked for the Ecclesiastical Commissioners, 'to examine and give his opinion upon all the plans sent in for the proposed public buildings.'

As a result of Christian's detailed report and recommendations the design of architects, Alexander & Henman, Stockton-On-Tees, Middlesborough, was accepted for the Town Hall. A sum of £240 was given to the successful competitors.

By November 1871 the Town Commissioners had received tenders for the erection of the building from various contractors, Messrs Trow & Son, Wednesbury, was given the contract to erect a town hall having submitted the lowest tender. Evidence shows that in January 1872, there was some dispute with Trow who refused to sign the contract due to the Commissioners attempting to reduce costs in respect of both the materials and labour.

The recorded minutes fail to disguise the heated arguments and blunt speaking that must have taken place between Trow and the members of the Committee. The crisis was, however, obviously resolved, for Trow completed his contract although, 'As the cost of the building is limited it has been necessary to use materials of an inexpensive description to keep the design as simple as is compatible with a certain character required in a Public Building.'

In October 1872 the Town Improvement Commissioners resolved to use common bricks at the back and side of the Town Hall instead of dressed bricks 'whereby savings were effected.'

Earlier that year, as a result of studying a report from the architects that there would be a space between the Hall and Lodge Road which would need to be fenced off, the Commissioners decided to pay an additional £75 to use that space as additional internal accommodation, 'when it was considered that by that course a considerable outlay for fencing will be saved.' But the Commissioners refused the architects' suggestion that the lighting in the retiring rooms should be from the side walls instead of the roof.

All records show that the Town Hall was built in brick and stone in an Italian Gothic Style and was erected 1874-1875. It was altered in 1905 to provide more offices and a Committee Room, and, in 1924 the Reading Room of the former Free Library building, next to the Town Hall, was converted into a Council Chamber.

In its issue 14 August 1875 the *West Bromwich Weekly News* gives the following detailed description of the exterior of this building.

The hall, which stands out prominently as the visitor enters the place either from the north or south sides of the district, stands on the corner site of the Lodge Estate, and has a frontage to the main road of about 130 feet. Externally the design is of bold proportions, having at the outer corner a massive tower rising to a height of over 130 feet, the upper stage being ornamented with a continuous arcade of detached columns, and trefoils arches, with a richly moulded cornice above, under the eaves of a high pitched roof broken up by large dormer windows, and a handsome group of chimneys on one side. From the front dormer is supported a lofty flagstaff. The tower stands slightly forward, and forms a very picturesque object, and can be seen a long distance off.

Below the arcading and around the tower circular openings are designed to receive an illuminated clock; but as yet nothing has been mooted with regard to the purchase of the indicator of the great enemy's pace.

Above the two side arches of the entrance, corbelled out from the wall, are bay windows with ornamental gablets, which pleasantly break up the main roof. The windows generally to the basement and ground floor have moulded stone lintels, and those of the first floor semi-circular arched heads of brick and red terracotta carving having an ornamental hood mould of the latest material, of which also the string courses, the cornices, arcading to tower etc. are made. Red pressed bricks are employed for the general facings, and green slates with red tile castings form the covering of the roofs.'

Many years later, in 1987, English Heritage made an assessment regarding the importance of the Town Hall as part of the heritage of West Bromwich with the result that it was granted the status of a Grade II Listed Building. (*Courtesy English Heritage List Description, English Heritage 1987*)

CHAPTER 2
THE BUILDING

The Town Hall's Main Entrance

The main entrance to the Town Hall has been described, in the 1875 edition of the *West Bromwich Weekly News*, as possessing, 'a strikingly noble frontage, under a triplet of well-proportioned arches, moulded and circled with chevron ornaments, and supported by stone columns, moulded bases and clustered carved capitals. Out of the angles of these are to be seen conventional foliage, spring heads, representing with charming fidelity the several months of the year.'

It is a matter of record that John Roddis was the sculptor of these carvings and the West Bromwich Town Improvement Commissioners were fortunate to employ his services. John Roddis was an accomplished sculptor who received many important commissions, for example, from the Earl of Carlisle at Castle Howard, to the Duke of Marlborough at Blenheim. Sir Gilbert Scott entrusted him with the execution of

between thirty and forty statues and statuettes for the Chapel of St Andrew in Gloucester Cathedral but alas, research has failed to reveal his plans or notes appertaining to the carving in our Town Hall. Any details or sketches regarding the design or concept of these icons remain elusive. Therefore, unless any future research reveals the actual plans, then the individual visitor to the Town Hall will have to reflect upon and decide their own interpretation of these personifications of the twelve months of the year.

The following comments may prove a fruitful platform to pursue future research. Professor George Noszlopy, University of Central England, kindly examined the carvings and made the following observations:

Stone Pillars, with carvings representing the months of the year, situated at the main entrance.

'The heads decorating the capitals of the clustered columns at the entrance

4

of West Bromwich Town Hall are personifications of the Months, and are inscribed with the names of the Months accordingly. Like the rest of the architectural sculpture on the building, they recall a medieval, mainly Norman Romanesque tradition of the Labours of the Months which often decorate the doorways of churches and cathedrals of the period in both England and the rest of Europe. The use of such architectural sculpture was motivated by the revivalist mentality of the second half of the nineteenth century, which was especially strong in the Midlands in both religious and civic life.'

Professor George Noszlopy's comments are reinforced by the foreword in the American book entitled *The Labors of the Months, In Antique & Mediaeval Art to the End of the Twelfth Century* by James Carson Webster.

'The Labors of the months is a theme of frequent occurrence in medieval art, a theme which is called to the attention of even the casual traveller by the presence in sculptural doorways of Romanesque churches and gothic cathedrals of those small vignettes in which bits of local and contemporary life find expression amid the sacred stories of Political history or awesome apocalyptic visions.'

Stone Pillars: a carving for the Month of September, an ear of corn in the hat represents harvest-time.

Professor Elizabeth McGrath, London, of the Warburg Institute, has also suggested that some of the Town Hall carvings may be 'whimsical' personifications of the Months of the Year. Examination of photographic files at the Institute, illustrating the tradition of using heads to symbolise months of the year, failed to produce carvings similar to those of West Bromwich Town Hall.

The Town Hall Tower and Spire
There seems to be something in the psychological makeup of the inhabitants of West Bromwich which attracts them to view the height of the Town Hall tower as an irresistible challenge to be faced and accepted at whatever the cost to themselves or others.

Local Councillor, Linda Turton, recounts the following story regarding H B Tuckey (1898 - 1941):

'Harold Benjamin Tuckey lost a leg in the First World War at the Battle of the Somme and he suffered from shell shock. A story is told that he climbed over the roof of the Town Hall in West Bromwich, with his one leg, thereby being the unwitting cause of the death of the Town Hall Caretaker. The poor caretaker saw a figure with one leg crawling over the glass sky-light and the shock was too much for him.'

Sam Chiles, a well known West Bromwich local historian, recounted the following anecdote about his time spent as a junior office boy in the Borough Treasurer's Office:

'Well, we did all sorts of things but what would interest you is the fact that while I was the office boy in 1927, they built a scaffolding round the Town Hall to do all the outside painting, the windows right up to the tower. This scaffolding went up, scaffolding and then platform, then ladders, scaffolding, platform, ladders and then at the very top they had put two ladders, right up from the highest platform to the weather vane. Of course, Joesbury, Dickinson and Brown challenged me to climb to the very top. I was really very scared but it was a challenge so up I went, ladder, platform, ladder, platform and when I got to the very top, there I was, practically level with the weather vane. There were regilding that, you know. In the weather vane, the wide part that catches the wind the date was cut out of the metal, 1873. Anyway, I climbed up, I was aged sixteen, and somebody saw me and they reported me to the Borough Treasurer. So, of course he had me in and gave me a real right dressing down and I remember he said, "It's not that you climbed it but you are not insured. The workmen are but you are not. I think I'll tell your father!" I said, "Oh don't do that!"

Well, years and years later, a long time after the war, my oppo was in charge of the loans and on the top floor of that building that runs from Lodge Road into Lombard Street, which had only got to be up for five years and it's still up, I was standing there, looking up at the tower and we'd got a new post office girl and she used to bring the post round in a pile and you'd got to sign for it.

I said, "Hey, come here. You've got good eyesight. There's some figures cut into that weather vane up there. I've often wondered what they are. See if you can decipher them."

She said, "I think that's a one, that's an eight, that's a seven. Is that a three or a five." I said, "I think that it is 1873!"

She replied, "Oh, haven't you got good eyesight Mr Chiles!"

"And she didn't know that I had been up there forty years ago!"

George Spencer, now living in Kent, whose father was engaged in stained-glass window making and worked for the firm of Martin Dunn's in West Bromwich recalled the following memory:

'My own Town Hall memories are few. The tower was visible from the window of the house in Izons Road - upstairs window that was in my bedroom - where I lived as a child. I have a vivid recollection of its being outlined with electric lights during, I think, a "Civic Week" in the early thirties. I would stand at the window gazing at it each night before I went to bed. It was something so unexpected and exotic in the familiar landscape.'

Finally, this story was told by Reg Thompson, who worked in the Town Hall from time to time during the 1940s and 1950s:

The selected design for the new Town Hall by the Architects, Messrs Alexander & Henman, of Stockton-on-Tees, Middlesborough. (The Building News 1871.)

'I used to go home on a bike but on this day I walked. When I walked back, the Town Hall spire was leaning over into Lodge Road. So, I told the guvnor and three of us went up and the bar beam that was holding the spire level had gone rotten on the end. Had it been left another twelve months it wouldn't have held out. We phoned over to the depot and the foreman came over and said, "What do you want to put it right?"

There were two of us working for three days. We used a car-jack and propped it all up and secured it. I don't know how we did it but we broke a slate at the bottom part of the spire and Mr Wood, who was then eighty-three, from Oldbury, a steeple –jack, walked up the roof.

I said, "Do you want a ladder?"

"No, I don't want a ladder my lad," he said, "I'm up there before you've fixed it!"

The Interior of the Town Hall

Members of the public attending various functions and events in the Town Hall are familiar with the well-worn flight of steps, with its central handrail, which allows them to gain access to the building but they probably rarely give any thought to the architecture of the interior of the Town Hall with its main hall and numerous doors leading into the corridor and its various adjoining rooms.

To recall the original purpose of the building compared to its use in the present day reveals a change in the social history and needs of the population since the Town Hall was erected in 1875.

The following information appeared in *The Building News*, 27 October 1871, regarding the selected design, with plans for the following rooms:

'Surveyor's Office; Inspector of Nuisances; Sub-Clerk's Office;
Rate Collector; Muniment Room; Retiring Rooms; Waiting Room;
Board Room; Clerk's Office; Committee Rooms; Cloakroom; WC's etc'

Nowadays, members of the general public seldom have an opportunity to enter these rooms which are now mainly offices that display the nameplates of important community functions such as Social Services, Library Services, and committee or conference rooms.

The emphasis has changed from the use of the building as the nucleus of the municipal life of the town to one that is the focal point for the integration of important services for the requirements of a modern society. Irrespective of the community and educational work that takes place within the building, not forgetting the provision for the leisure and social pursuits of the population, it is interesting to consider the actual architecture and decoration of its interior.

The Main Hall

The decorations in the interior of the main hall retain the Victorian interest in Gothic or Medieval architecture. An article in the *West Bromwich Weekly News,* August 1875, describes the hall as follows:

'Two stone staircases beside the main staircase lead to the Galleries, which are continued around three sides of the hall. At one end is a recessed orchestra, with a moveable platform in front.

The roof is supported by semi-circular cast-iron principals, resting upon cast-iron columns, which also form the supports for the galleries. The ceilings, the iron work, the walls, the floors of the hall and the pillars have been richly and lavishly decorated (from designs by the architect) by Mr S Broadbank, of Stockton-on-Tees. The harmonious blending of colours, and the magnificent stencil work, costing many days of artistic and patient labour, cannot be too highly praised, and words can hardly express the charming effect that they have produced.' (*Plate I iv*)

The Stained Glass Windows

When entering the Town Hall by the main entrance in the High Street, to the right of the corridor, there are some large stained glass windows situated by the main staircase. These windows are worth more than a cursory glance by people who ascend the stone stairs to gain access to the upper floor or gallery in the main hall.

The design of the large stained glass windows may not look impressive when compared to those of other public buildings, but when sunlight shines through them it illuminates and enhances the colours and design, thus transforming that whole area. (*Plate I i*)

The central window panel in particular deserves a more detailed examination as its crest represents an example of the town's trade and industry of a bygone age.

Research into the window's central design has proved a tantalising, if somewhat fascinating trail to follow. One suggestion was that the North Staffordshire Improvement Commissioners financed the windows, and so the kilns in the crest could be representing the bottle-ovens used for pottery but so far there is no evidence to support this theory.

It would be quite an achievement if, at some future date, plans or literature became available to solve this little mystery. The following points of view may be of interest and shed some light on the subject. Fortunately, some historians in our midst kindly spared the time to offer their opinion about the crest or legend in the central window.

John M Day, retired Town Clerk (1945-1973), stated that he had been told that the stained glass windows represented the Arms of the North Staffordshire

Improvement Commissioners and during his term of office he had asked numerous people but they did not know.

Stanley Shakespeare, who lived in West Bromwich but now resides in London, recognised the window crest and made the following observations:

'The buildings depicted in the window represent, two bottle kilns either side of an early brick built iron furnace in the centre. The name 'Bottle-Kiln' refers to the shape not the use. They were either for pottery or glass.'

By a strange coincidence, on the same day, John Brimble, a local historian, immediately recognised the middle building (from a photograph) and stated 'the large structure shown is a representation of a blast furnace, obviously representing the local iron industry of the time.'

The Curator at the Gladstone Pottery Museum in Stoke-on-Trent, when viewing a copy of the crest, suggested that 'the images were bottle-ovens which are associated with the late nineteenth century or early twentieth century kilns and that they could be bottle-ovens but on a balance of probabilities they could be glass ovens or cones, that is, given the local glass industry in the area.'

This opinion was reinforced by Roger Dodworth, Keeper of Glass and Fine Art, at Broadfield House Glass Museum in Kingswinford, who produced a picture of a lithograph of Chance Brothers Spon Lane Works, West Bromwich, 1857, in the firm's publication, *Mirror for Chance*, published for the 1951 Festival of Britain, in which the shape of the glass kilns mirror those in the crest in the stained glass window in West Bromwich Town Hall.

Finally, the search to confirm the design of the crest must end with an 1875 report from the *West Bromwich Weekly News*, which recorded that:

'The main staircase is lighted by large windows filled with stained glass, in the centre panel of which is the newly adopted crest and motto of the Commissioners. The crest is appropriately enough represented by a blast furnace and two ovens, one on either side. Encircling it is the motto *Labor Omnia Vincit* and underneath is the Staffordshire knot. The stained glass was supplied by Messrs. Dunn and Broughall.' (*Plate I iii*)

It is fitting that a local firm supplied the stained glass for the windows as they were 'glass and lead merchants, oil, colour and varnish merchants, High Street' and were well qualified to do so, according to their entry in various editions of *Kelly's Staffordshire Directory*. This report implies that everything was under the control of the West Bromwich Town Improvement Commissioners but it fails to answer the question as to who actually designed the crest or who financed the stained glass windows, although the 'Minutes Book 2', dated August 1872, refers to a loan for the purpose of erecting buildings, which includes the Town Hall.

George Spencer, already referred to (on page 7), has a catalogue of stained glass window designs published by Martin Dunn, West Bromwich, which appears to date from the turn of the 20th Century. The designs are described as 'registered' and records that the firm was established in 1861.

George's father, also named George Spencer (1886-1970), was a stained glass window craftsman who, in the 1940s, worked at Martin Dunn's in High Street. At that time the firm designed the stained glass windows it supplied, one of the designers being William (Bill) Leddington. Therefore, it may be safe to assume that the original stained glass window and crest in the Town Hall was in fact designed by Dunn and Broughall of West Bromwich, unless of course it was only built by them to a design of the original architects Alexander & Henman. So the mystery continues to this day.

CHAPTER 3
SECRETS OF THE CORRIDORS

It is amazing how often one can 'look without seeing' and this is never more true than when applied to the countless visitors, whatever their age, who pass through the portals of the Town Hall. If they pause, however, for only a moment or two to study the contents of the corridors then they will be amply rewarded with some fascinating facts about the history of the building.

On entering the main corridor it is interesting to note and examine in detail the exhibits and wall decorations. These span the years from the present day, represented by the photographic displays and information about the Sandwell Borough Youth Orchestra's success and impressive achievements, both locally and nationally, to travelling back in time to three Charters displayed on the wall in the main corridor which are:

Charter of Grant of Arms made to the County Borough of West Bromwich
13th September 1882;
Charter of the Grant of Arms made to the Borough of Wednesbury
10th July 1886;
Charter of the Grant of Arms made to the Borough of Tipton
10th September 1938.

The Charter of Incorporation (1882)
It is interesting to consider briefly the background to the granting of this Charter. The petition for obtaining a Charter was the result of discussions at several meetings of the Improvement Commissioners when they considered the implications of the Municipal Corporation Act, 1877 and its advantages to the town. (ref: Minute Bk 5 – Accounts Book-17/4201)

A public meeting in the Town Hall, on 25 January 1882, was well attended and the inhabitants of the town passed a resolution that the Improvement Commissioners should take steps to obtain a charter. It was recorded in the Minutes:

'That the Petition of the inhabitant householders of West Bromwich to the Queen in Council to grant a Charter of Incorporation for the parish of West Bromwich creating it a Municipal Borough under the Municipal Corporation (New Charter) Act 1877 be sealed with the Common Seal.'

F W Hackwood, in his book *A History of West Bromwich* sets out a list of advantages and benefits to the citizens for the town to become a municipal borough. He also recorded the arguments in support of the petition at the Privy Council official enquiry held in the Town Hall. However, the sentiments which appeals most may be his comments that:

> 'There was no disposition whatever to find fault with the government of the Commissioners; but there was an avowed and laudable aspiration for the enjoyment of the very highest form of municipal life possible.'

Therefore, due to the status of the town being elevated to that of a municipal borough; the ever vigilant Town Improvement Commissioners anticipated the need for:

> 'A Common Seal for the proposed Borough of West Bromwich which borough may assume amorial bearings to be duly enrolled in the Herald's College..... As it will take some time to obtain a Grant of Arms your Committee consider it prudent to instruct the Clerk to apply to Herald's College for a Grant of Arms at a cost of £76-10-0 immediately the Municipal Charter is received.' (Minute Book 5 - Account Book Feb 1882-July 1884)

The Board of Commissioners decided to adopt the second of two designs submitted by the College of Heralds and the motto *Labor Omnia Vincit* (labour conquers all things). There are several interpretations of this motto and that quoted above is provided by the local Community History Archives Service (CHAS) and confirmed by the College of Arms, London, who also stated that the 1st Earl Attlee, Labour Prime Minister in 1945, adopted this motto.

On the wall of the main corridor, in a prominent position, there is an important document, namely, The Charter of the Grant of Arms, for the Municipal Borough of West Bromwich (1882). (*Plate III ii*)

Coat of Arms, West Bromwich
Arms granted in 1882.
Motto: LABOR OMNIA VINCIT
Crest: stag and ostrich feathers from arms of Earls of Dartmouth.
Shield: stag's head representing Earls of Dartmouth; mullets (stars) and fleur-de-lys around border represents Sandwell Hall, ancestral home of the Dartmouths; gold millrinds (clamps found at the centres of mill wheels) symbolise metal-based industries.
Description: These arms were granted to West Bromwich in 1882. Except the millrinds which represent the iron and brass foundries, the emblems are all derived

from the arms, crest and supporters of the Earls of Dartmouth, who were formally seated at Sandwell Hall. (*reference: Community History Archives Service*) (*Plate IV i*)

The Passage of Time

In an inconspicuous corner of the main corridor stands an important cabinet pendulum clock which has witnessed many of the inevitable 'high and lows', successes and disappointments of life within the borough.

George Taylor, for many years a West Bromwich Corporation electrician, recently recalled his memories about the clocks in the Town Hall.

The Face in the Crowd by George Taylor

'Since its opening day in 1875, West Bromwich Town Hall must have had millions of people visiting, attending functions, dances, shows and weddings amongst many other forms of entertainment.

Probably its most frequent visitors were from the local borough and its surrounding towns. But one face that has seen history unfolding in the walls of this magnificent hall, and always in the same place, is the face of the Town Hall clock!

How many people have actually looked after the clock since its installation, I do not know. I can however recall the person who maintained it from the mid-seventies, up to nineteen-ninety. His name was Steve Artess, who like myself worked for West Bromwich Corporation from the early seventies.

When the clocks around the Town Hall complex were first installed, the master clock situated in the main corridor, controlled and kept time for all of the other 'slave' clocks. Unfortunately, these clocks over the years, have suffered the fate of neglect, and of course fashion. There are now only four clocks plus the master clock remaining. One that I have mentioned is at the rear of the main hall. One is in the Council Chamber, one in Committee Room "A", and the other in a room used by the Library. Several repairs have been carried out to the master clock over the years, until maintenance was stopped in the late eighties. This almost led to its demise. The master clock was subject to an attack of vandalism

Master Pendulum Clock, Electric Synchronome, made in England, situated in the main corridor.

in 1993/1994 and I was called upon to repair it. The front glass was replaced and the case was repaired, but the interior mechanism, being of a delicate nature did not work again until extensive and painstaking repairs were carried out by myself. Fortunately the maintenance contract was re-instated and the remaining clocks are now all in working order.'

Fallen Heroes - The Boer War (1899-1902)

Perhaps one of the 'lows' the Town Hall commemorates is reflected in the copper plaque honouring those who fell in the Boer War. This plaque is situated above the doors which lead into the main hall. The reflection of the corridor lights upon its surface, plus its age and height, make the inscription impossible to decipher from the ground. It took the combined efforts of Paul Wise the Curator, and Jim Hayes, the Mayor's ex-Chauffeur, to decipher this citation, which was accomplished with the aid of stepladders, a steady pair of hands plus a pencil and writing-pad! The inscription is as follows (*Plate III iii*):

THIS TABLET IS ERECTED BY THE MAYOR ALDERMEN & BURGESSES
OF THIS BOROUGH TO COMMEMORATE THE DEVOTION OF THE MEN OF THIS
TOWN WHOSE NAMES ARE HEREAFTER INSCRIBED TO THE SERVICE OF
THEIR SOVEREIGN AND COUNTRY IN VOLUNTARILY OFFERING THEMSELVES
FOR SERVICE & SERVING WITH THE FORCES IN THE FIELD IN THE BOER WAR
WHICH COMMENCED THE 11TH OCTOBER 1899 & ENDED MAY 31ST 1902.
CHARLES JOHN CADDICK MB

SGT. WILLIAM. M. SMITH	BUCKS YEOMANRY	WILLIAM HENRY COLE
L/CPL CHARLES. P. DEWSON	MAJ. THOMAS PARISH (KILLED IN ACTION)	ERNEST BAYLISS
THOMAS HABLE	1ST EAST KENT YEOMANARY	THOMAS CALLEAR
GEORGE ERNEST NEALE	HENRY HAMMOND	JOSEPH WARD
PVT. JOHN. P. THOMAS	WILTSHIRE YEOMANARY	THOMAS TAYLOR
WILLIAM ALFRED PHILLIPS	JOHN CLIFFORD M.C. ILWRAITH	PERCY. J. PARSONS
SAMUEL HERBERT MANIFOLD	DIED ON ACTIVE SERVICE	HORACE CLEMANCE QUANCE
WILLIAM JAMES EDWARDS	MIDDLESEX YEOMANRY	THOMAS BUNN
ARCHIBALD SMITH	FREDRICK WILLIAM KIDDLE	ALBERT SHINTON
GEORGE. H. BEALE	JOHN ANSTEY?	FRANK NAYLOR
SYDNEY DARBY	IMPERIAL YEOMANRY	1ST E & K COMPANIES
ALLEN HASSELL	FREDRICK JOHN SIDDENS	1ST VOLUNTARY SOUTH
WILLIAM. C. WOODHALL	WARWICKSHIRE YEOMANRY	STAFFORDSHIRE REGIMENT
	CPL. D. J. PARKES	
	BRABAMPS HORSE	

HMS *Bermuda* (1939 – 1945)

The passage of time and sadly, another war, is represented in the corridor by a wooden shield which bears the badge of HMS *Bermuda*. This badge was presented by the Lord Commissioners of the Admiralty to West Bromwich to commemorate the Borough's adoption of HMS *Bermuda* during World War II (1939 – 1945).

'The badge of HMS *Bermuda* represents a demi-lion affronte erased red holding in the dexter paw a trident also red on a white background. It is based on the Arms of Bermuda. The Bermuda flag has the same creature in the same colour.' (Source: Imperial War Museum) (*Plate IV iv*)

Corridor Floor Tiles

To the casual observer the well worn, often faded patterned floor tiles in the Town Hall corridors are probably accepted as familiar but unexciting remnants of a bygone age. There is usually a total disregard of the colours and variety of designs of these floor tiles as they are seen merely as a pathway which lead to a variety of rooms within the building. A little time spent delving into the manufacture of these tiles, however, makes them take on a new significance and suddenly they become a precious link with the past, both social and industrial.

The *West Bromwich Weekly News*, August 1875 recorded:

'A flight of steps twelve feet in width gives access from the principal entrance to a corridor nine feet wide, laid with a handsome encaustic tile pavement by Messrs. Maw & Co.' (*Plate II i*)

To describe this newly laid floor as 'handsome' immediately fires the imagination to an appreciation of how rich the colours and patterns must have looked in those far-off days. However, some difficulty occurs in understanding the unfamiliar term, 'an encaustic tile pavement'

A visit to the Jacksfield Tile Museum at Ironbridge, on an extremely cold winter's day, was amply rewarded by the warm greetings and interest of the Museum Staff. Even more rewarding was the news that the photograph of the Town Hall's 'encaustic tile pavement' showed that they were definitely manufactured at the Ironbridge site. The following texts from the Museum provide some background information into the history of encaustic tiles manufactured by Maw & Co.

Maw & Co. Ltd - Encaustic and geometric floor tiles

These tiles were made at the company's Benthall Works, close to the Iron Bridge, the Ironbridge Gorge, Shropshire. Maw & Co. was a family business owned by a wealthy retired businessman, and run by his sons, George and Arthur.

The brothers' combined knowledge of design and understanding of production techniques enabled the business to flourish.

In the late 1870's work began on Maw & Co.'s purpose built factory in Jackfield village, also in the Gorge. When the works were complete in 1883 the new tile works was the largest of its kind in the world. Maw & Co. boasted an international reputation and were widely recognised as leaders of the Victorian tile industry.

After the 1840's designers and architects began to use medieval styles in their work, thus prompting a period of architectural design termed the Gothic Revival. Early Victorian encaustic tile design was taken from medieval heraldic design and patterns, this allowed for their extensive use in the repair of medieval buildings.

The Clay
The early encaustic tiles were made in a limited colour range, due to the differential contraction of the different coloured clays which formed cracks in the design.

The most common design of red body clay with white pattern inlay had least difficulties with the clay shrinking during firing. Black and buff tiles were also common. *(Text and information courtesy of Ironbridge Gorge Museum Trust)*

A closer examination of the Town Hall corridor tiles reinforced the opinion that they were indeed encaustic, that is "inlaid with coloured clays burnt in" *(The Concise Oxford Dictionary-Fifth Edition 1964)*. However, the icing on the cake proved to be the discovery that the actual design and colour of the tiles were advertised in an original *Maw & Co* pattern catalogue that is in the collection of the Ironbridge Gorge Museum Trust *(Plate II ii)*. Although the catalogue is in a fragile condition due to its age, the Library Staff kindly took some photographs which show the plate and pattern number of the tiles.

**Weights & Measures Act
by John M Day**
A brass rule was let into the floor along the edge of the Town Hall's main corridor as an Imperial Standard Measurement. At set intervals brass plates marked out the following measurements from 0ft; 10ft; 20ft; 33ft; 50ft; and 66ft.

Brass rule plate, one of a set of six plates laid in the main corridor floor at fixed intervals. Each brass plate is stamped with an Imperial Standard Measurement from 0ft to 66ft.

CHAPTER 4
SECRETS OF THE ROOMS

As the main artefacts in the corridors have disclosed some of their secrets and involvement in the distinguished history of the town, perhaps it is appropriate to examine the various rooms leading from these corridors.

The principal rooms of 1875 were described in the *West Bromwich Weekly News* as follows:

> 'Opening from the corridor are porters lobby, waiting room, surveyor's office and offices for the sub-clerk, rate collector, inspector of nuisances. The muniment room, which is of fire-proof construction and fitted with a Milner's fire-proof door opens out of the Surveyors Office.'

During the following years these rooms have been used, added to and altered to suit the requirements of each particular era. However, the general public would be aware of four main offices in particular, namely, the Borough Treasurer's Office, the Rates Office, the Council Chamber and, in particular, the Mayor's Parlour. Sam Chiles recalls:

> 'At the back of the Town Hall, towards the Lodge Road, there was what we used to call the Retiring Room. It was a big room, on the ground floor, divided into two by a partition, which used to go in to the ceiling (and at the time of the dancing they used that as a bar).
>
> The doorway which leads on to the balcony in the Town Hall has a door that has been moved since then, it used to go further down. That doorway was moved because on the wall in the old days there was a huge map, which showed all the pits, mines and roads in West Bromwich a hundred years ago.
>
> When you come to a door by the balustrade there is a narrow flight of stairs. On your left on the wall is a trap door and just inside is a narrow flight of stairs. You can walk along the gangway above the ceiling of the hall itself and that's where they go on Armistice Day and throw the poppies down.'

The following reminiscence recalls a visit to the Town Hall in the 1930s and was submitted by an anonymous contributor.

'My first memories of the Town Hall would be about 1936 to 1939, when it was the sort of place you only went in to if you really had to! It seemed that sort of place to me at that time, overwhelming.

The first time I remember actually going into the place would be about the end of 1936, when my mother took me with her to renew my father's Motor Vehicle Licence. It was quite an ordeal, first there was the Form to be obtained from the Town Hall, there was quite a queue for this, and the Clerk would hand it over as if it were gold!

This was taken home and filled in by father and together with the form and appropriate money we returned to the Town Hall.

It was usually a morning's work to renew the Road Tax as the queue stretched out of the office (turn left on entering, then first office on the left) and it was not unknown to reach the main entrance to the Hall. One man used to specialise in issuing Road Tax Discs, it was Mr Hare, and he operated from a closed partition at the end of the room so that you could not see what was going on! He was a very meticulous man and the smallest error on the Form and it was rejected (no alterations allowed), which meant joining a queue for a replacement Form and starting the whole process again the next day. It seemed as if when the end of December came nearer the queues got longer.

Kids could not "run around", you had to stand still, by your parent or the Hall Caretaker would be "having a word" with you, with threats of having to leave the queue!'

As a contrast to the above account, it is interesting to hear about life in the Borough Treasurer's Office from the point of view of someone who actually worked there and once more Sam Chiles recalled memories of his working life in the office.

The Borough Treasurer's Office by Sam Chiles

'I went to the Borough Treasurer's Office in 1927 upon leaving the Grammar School. I'd got to start on Monday, 1 August 1927 but it was a Bank Holiday. So Monday and Tuesday I didn't work but as I got paid from the 1 August I had two days paid holiday to start with. I was the office boy for about twelve months and when I joined the office I was the thirtieth member. I can recall everyone's names and the Borough Treasurer was Mr Wilson. I used to have to work at a little private counter. The big counter was there and there was a partition and a little counter where people came who wanted to have their meter emptied and all that sort of thing.

"What's your name and address?" I would write in a book and then tear the paper out and pass it on to whoever had got to deal with it. I used to just run about for everybody.

Anyway, I went there on the Wednesday and nobody told me anything. To find out what time we finished I looked at the gas accounts and it said that the office hours were two to four. I thought I'd got to go home at 4pm. But I waited for everyone else to go. They went at 5pm. So I went home, too.

In those days everybody paid their money over to the cashiers, e.g. the Rent Collectors, the Meter Men. They used to come up with £10 worth of copper you know, five or six of them. The Transport paid over to the Cashier and he put it behind the counter. Well, you can imagine, on the Wednesday of holiday week there were the Saturday takings, the Sunday takings, the Monday takings and the Tuesday takings from transport. There were dozens of £5 of copper in those bags in the old days and hundreds of pounds of silver. He'd got a stack of those behind the counter and they'd all got to go down to the strong room to be locked up at night in the basement.

But nobody told me; so at quarter–past five I went home and the next morning did I have a rousting off Mr Phillips. He and Mr Randle, the Assistant Borough Treasurer, walked up and down to the strong room twenty or thirty times carrying this money. Nobody told me!

Then Mr Phillips told me, "You've got to take this money downstairs into the strong room and lock it up."

Then when we'd finished and balanced it we would take the money down and then together we'd lock two doors on the strong room. Then the next morning he'd call me and he'd go and pay the money into the bank. So, I'd got to carry all those bags from the strong room to the bank, journey, after journey, after journey. You can imagine how much money there was that day. Mr Phillips and Mr Randall nearly killed themselves, I think, carrying them down to the strong room. Well. They couldn't tell me off because they hadn't given me any instructions.

Wages were always recorded in big wages books e.g. the highways, education, caretakers, transport, housing. They had big wages' books to fill in the names and the hours and they used to bring them up to the Town Hall on a Wednesday or Thursday. They used to go to audit them then they went into Mr Griffith's office for the wages to be drawn and checked what to get out of the bank to put in the packets. Well, I fell down those stairs with three or four wages' books. I thought I was strong you see and I was carrying them down the stairs to get onto the subway and I fell down these (bloody) stairs with these books. That knocked me out a bit but coming down the other way one day, the ceiling comes down low, and instead of walking down the last two steps I jumped down them and hit my head on the corner and that knocked me out!

In those days Mr Wickham was the Town Clerk. I was a boy so I had to visit all the departments. It was half-past five so I went up those stairs like a greyhound and this Mr Wickham was going up the stairs. I went round him doing two or three steps at a time.

"Boy!" he yelled, "Don't you ever let me see you doing that again! Don't you understand the amount of barometric pressure that is building up on your body?"

This account of handling heavy wages books and rushing round visiting various departments during a working day shows how much technology has advanced since those early days in the Treasurers Office. Today's society, and especially the workforce, has progressed to a more technological age with the use of sophisticated telecommunications, such as computers, emails and fax machines.

At times, the Offices of Borough Treasurer and Borough Surveyor require action to be taken over and above the call of duty. Although not strictly within the terms of their job description, particular talents are called upon to resolve unforeseen circumstances which occur from time to time. The following incidents demonstrate when it was vital for these guardians of the town to possess a sense of humour.

Sam Chiles reminiscences includes the following account in which he draws attention to the degree of co-ordination, or lack of it, between the various departments within the Town Hall.

The Borough Surveyor's Tarmac Incident

'The Borough Surveyor and the Electrical Engineer fell out because in those days, if the Borough Surveyor was going to tarmac a street, the first thing he would do was to get in touch with the electricity department and say, "Are you going to do any work in Beeches Road?" where he lived.

"Do you want to do any work at Beeches Road with the electricity?"
Gas, Water Works, he'd ring round and finally he phoned round and said,

"I want to do the road but not if you have any work to do!"

"Oh, no!" they all said.

So, he had Beeches Road tarmacked and made a good job of it.
About two or three months later the Electrical Engineer came along and he wanted to put new cables down as the electricity was DC then and if you were on the end of the circuit you didn't get much light. Now it is AC.

So, they sent a man around, you know Surveyors, and the Borough Surveyor said, " I asked you if you wanted to do any work in Beeches Road and you said, "No! So you are not going to break my tarmac up!"

So, they argued about it and then the Surveyor had an idea.

"I'll tell you what we are going to do. You can put the cable in the gutter under the monkey bricks."

So, he put the cable right down in Beeches Road.

About twenty or thirty years later the electricity people were all over Beeches Road. looking for this cable. They dug up holes all over the road but they couldn't find it.

Some old bloke, about ninety years old, stood there watching and he said, "What are you blokes looking for?"

"Well, of course, the bad language came out!

We're looking for this …… cable!"

He said, "Well, I can tell you exactly where it is."

They looked at each other and said. "He's round the bend!"

He repeated, "I can tell you exactly where it was put down. I remember it very well."

So, they said, "Where is it then?"

He said, "Under the monkey bricks."

And they dug them up and there it was, under the monkey bricks!'

The Borough Surveyor's Dilemma (or the secret of the pigs)

As the story related above shows, it is not always an easy task carrying out the duties of Office. Reg Thompson's revelations below give some insight, not only to the difficulties of supervising the workforce 'off site' from the confines of a base at the Town Hall, but it also shows a bit of that entrepreneurial spirit that existed during the war years.

'There was thirteen of us on duty at the Work's Department and I must admit that we were the biggest rogues that God put on this earth! They used to call us the 'bacon squad' because we used to get bacon from places that nobody else knew of.

The boss decided that he wanted a pig-sty building, so, we built him a pig-sty in the Corporation yard and the yard man looked after the pigs. He had two and they were beauties. It was nothing for him to come and say that he'd got half a dozen fowl and there was a pigeon loft and we had pigeon pie one night. Oh, they used to go raving mad! "Who's done this, and who's done that?"

But the funny part about it - I wasn't there, but my brother said that the Corporation decided that they would like to put on a concert in the Town Hall for all the people who take part in the ARP. So they did, but some crafty devil tipped the comedian off about these pigs and he blarted it all out at this concert. The Surveyor was there and heard it and he went stark raving mad! They said that he was in the yard the next morning and he stood there while they knocked the pig-sty down.'

The Council Chamber (*Plate III i*)

In 1924 the reading room of the former free library building next to the Town Hall was converted into a Council Chamber. This room is situated at the end of the main corridor, through a door which has a leaded-light window designed with the West Bromwich Coat of Arms. (*Plate I i*)

The Council Chamber has a public gallery near a door that leads directly on to High Street. On the wall, opposite this gallery, is the Coat of Arms of the Borough and three wooden boards which record names and organisations which have been honoured by the Borough in recognition of their services to the town. These boards display the following information:

Roll of Mayors of West Bromwich, The names of all the Mayors are inscribed on this board.

Roll of Freemen of the Borough, lists the names of people who received this honour from the Borough in recognition of their services to the town.

Roll of Freedom of Entry to the Borough, which entitles the named regiments to march through the town with fixed bayonets.

The *Evening Mail*, in 1964, recorded the fact that the 904 Company, RASC (TA) based at Carter's Green, was granted the Freedom of the Borough and the unit had to obtain special permission from the Ministry of Defence to wear a badge of the town's Coat of Arms on their tunics.

Memories of a Town Hall Ceremony by Eileen Hadgkiss, from Somerset.

'I have many memories from my childhood, growing up in West Bromwich, and then Great Bridge where we moved in 1949, but I have no family there now, even so I love to hear about the town, obviously more about the

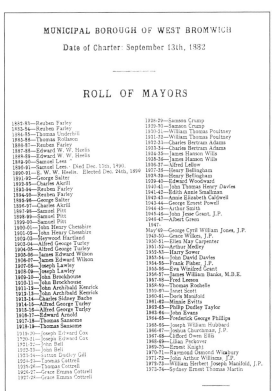

Roll of Mayors, 1882 – 1974, in the Council Chamber.

Boards showing the Roll of Freemen and the Roll of Mayors of West Bromwich, situated in the Council Chamber.

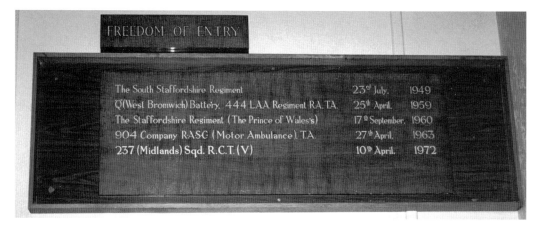

A third Council Chamber board displays the Roll of Freedom of Entry to the County Borough of West Bromwich, from 23 July 1949 to 10 April 1972.

past than the present. Some time between 1934 / 1939 my late father who was a Bugler in the TA at Carter's Green Drill Hall, had to attend a ceremony outside the Town Hall. A platform had been built across the pavement for the dignitaries to stand on, with my father in one corner, whilst another soldier stood in the opposite one. They had to play bugle calls, except that the other chap couldn't play, so while dad blew the calls the other fellow had to pretend. Dad always used to say that he lost a days pay, and was never paid for the duty he performed. No doubt somewhere there is a record of this ceremony. Certainly there was a photo taken because we had a copy at home.'

John M Day, retired Town Clerk, was instrumental in creating a unique ceremony in the Council Chamber as he suggested that,

'The Bell of HMS *Bermuda* should be installed in the Council Chamber and rung at the beginning and end of formal Council Meetings. After Sandwell took over, the tradition was abandoned and the Bell was presented to the West Bromwich Royal Naval Association.'

The Mayor's Parlour
This domain of the once powerful First Citizen of the Town is barely an echo of its former glory with a lack of furnishings robbing it of atmosphere or a sense of its importance in the history of the borough.

The remnants of the town's heritage remain in the carvings over the open fire – place and in the sturdy Mayoral oak chair, with its wooden carving depicting the crest and industry of the town. The bar in the Mayor's Parlour is, perhaps, a reminder of the role this room played in dispensing hospitality to the frequent and important guests of the borough. Perhaps this bare, insignificant room can recapture its reputation, if not its grandeur, in the memories it evokes in the citizens of the town. (*Plate IV ii*)

CHAPTER 5
FOR THE GLORY OF THE TOWN

The Town Improvement Commissioners Minutes record the members concern over, 'the continued delay' in finishing the building of the Town Hall and that they had seriously considered the option of transferring the work to a firm 'independent of the contractors.' However, all the problems were eventually resolved after many months of frustration, due to delays and lack of progress by the contractors and the work was completed to everyone's satisfaction. The *Daily Gazette 1875,* reported:

> 'The hall has been, it is true, a long time in course of erection; but, now that it is finished, it shows much careful labour bestowed upon it, and it is, in every sense, a place which the inhabitants may with justice admire.'

At long last, the scene was set for the inhabitants of the town to celebrate the completion of this "architectural triumph", which was officially handed over to the Town's Improvement Commissioners. It was decided that the Town Hall would be formally opened on the 10 August 1875.

> 'Mr. Reuben Farley, Chairman of the Commissioners, generously decided to mark this auspicious occasion with a Banquet, to be held in the new prestigious Town Hall. Invitations were issued to 'most of the public bodies in the town, including these gentlemen who gave their time and attention to public duties.' (*West Bromwich Weekly News,* 1875).

An irate citizen who criticised the guest list and made some scathing comments upon the selection of guests sent a letter of dissension to one Editor. However, the article in the *West Bromwich Weekly News* pre-empted such outrageous criticism with the assertion that:

> 'In the language of a correspondent last week we would say, 'surely such a representative yet comprehensive list should knock the bottom out of any charge of exclusiveness and ought to satisfy all reasonable men of the Chairman's Catholicity in his hospitality.'
>
> The Chairman did not forget the ladies and invitations were issued to them for coffee at six o'clock, and from the galleries they had the privilege of viewing the 'lords of creation' and listening to the speeches.'

Alderman Reuben Farley, (b.1826 d.1899), was the first Mayor of West Bromwich.
Photographer: Sidney Darby, West Bromwich. With kind permission of Tony Usherwood.

Thus, the Board of Commissioners and other illustrious guests prepared to enjoy and celebrate the completion of the long-awaited fruits of their labours.

The Banquet, 10 August, 1875

It does not require a vivid imagination to visualise the scene on the evening of the Banquet, which was held to celebrate the opening of the Town Hall. It is tempting to speculate about the great air of expectancy and immense excitement generated on this auspicious occasion but it is more interesting, perhaps, to recall the events of the day as recorded by those who actually witnessed this great milestone in the life of the town.

'A large and fashionable company assembled at six o'clock, when the road immediately between Christ Church to the Public Buildings was literally blocked with spectators, who all seemed anxious to catch a glimpse of the personages who alighted from their carriages in front of the Town Hall. A small body of police was on the spot, who effectively prevented any possible disorder or indecorum. Early in the morning the bells of Christ Church were ringing, and the national flag was hoisted on the tower of the hall.

The fine, spacious hall was appropriately decorated; the orchestra, which was occupied by Messrs Synyer and Gilmer's band, assuming a very pretty appearance. During the evening the band enlivened the proceedings by giving in the most artistic manner, a selection of operatic music.'
(*West Bromwich Weekly News*, 14 August 1875)

The 'sumptuous banquet' lasted about two hours and there followed the inevitable speeches, responses and toasts to the Queen; the Earl of Dartmouth and all honoured guests. A well-deserved speech of thanks and a toast was made to "The Chairman" who in response said,

'As a native of West Bromwich he had striven, and should still strive, to the end of his days to do what he could towards the advancement of the town. (loud applause) He would again thank them heartily for the honour which they had done him.' (*West Bromwich Weekly News*, 14 August 1875)

This banquet was the first of many celebrations to mark an important era in the history of the town but it was also an extremely significant occasion because it was during the after dinner speeches that, in the words of a local historian, 'Mr. Alexander Brogden, at that time M.P. for the Borough of Wednesbury, in which West Bromwich was then comprehended generously offered to present a gift of an organ for this magnificent hall.'

The Incorporation Banquet, 7 December 1882
Seven years later, in 1882, another banquet was held in the Town Hall to celebrate the town being given the status of a municipal borough by being granted a Charter of Incorporation. This auspicious occasion was acknowledged in the General Purposes Committee report of the Town Council,

'Your Committee have resolved to have the front of the Public Buildings illuminated on the occasion of the banquet given by the Mayor, to celebrate the Incorporation of the Borough, on the 7th proximo.'

Unfortunately, the Council had no control over the atrocious weather for a heavy fall of snow a few days before the banquet made the roads almost impassable and a cold wind plus the damp atmosphere nearly ruined the spectacular illuminations and decorations outside the Town Hall and along High Street.

Although not strictly within the remit of this research perhaps it would be appropriate to mention that *The Free Press*, 9 December 1882, described the illuminations and decorations surrounding the Town Hall as follows:

'Such a wealth of bunting has surely been but rarely seen along the High Street of West Bromwich. (with) a row of flags across Dartmouth Street to Sandwell Road, (and) a perfect cluster of flags between the Town Hall and Spon Lane. Coming to the more special designs, which comprehended a large number of gas illuminations, the making and fixing of which has occupied the attention of an increased staff of men from the Corporation Gas Department almost night and day during the last fortnight.

The illumination of the municipal buildings was on a most elaborate scale. Over the High Street entrance to the Town Hall was a copy of the Borough Arms, with a nine foot crown on the right and a nine ft plume, with the motto, on the left; under the crown, "V.R.," and under the plume, "A.E.," in six –foot letters...... Mr. Parker, of the Birmingham House, made the corner of New Street resplendent with the words, "Success to the Borough," in gas letters three feet in height. Messrs. Dunn and Broughall showed two six feet stars, with the letters, "V.R." between. Outside the Free Press Company's Stationary Warehouse in High Street was shown the largest single gas device in the town, being a correct copy of the Borough Arms, 11ft.6in. by 8ft. in size. Under the shield is a ribbon bearing the motto *Labor omnia vincit* translated as 'Labour overcomes everything.' *(translation by CHAS and confirmed as correct by The Herald's College, London May 2002)*

There must have been a tremendous atmosphere of anticipation both outside the Town Hall as well as within its hallowed portals on that special evening. It was an occasion when the full splendour and the richness of the Civic Regalia were in evidence to enhance what was described as a 'brilliant' gathering.

The Mayor (Alderman Reuben Farley) wore the Chain of Office for the first time and the silver Mace, given to the Borough by the Mayor, occupied a place worthy of its magnificence on the table in front of him. It would appear that a formal presentation of the Chain of Office and the Silver Mace was made to the Mayor and Corporation at a later date because at a Council Meeting, held in the Council Chamber on 3 January 1883, when the following letter from the Earl of Dartmouth was read:

"Patshull, January 1st 1883.

"My dear Mr. Mayor,
"I beg to make hereby the formal presentation to the Mayor and Corporation of West Bromwich, the Mayoral Chain to be worn by the Mayor of that Borough during his term of Office, and at the same time to assure you formally, but with great satisfaction, that your own treatment of myself in a matter as to which we took opposite views that suggested to me the thought of offering this chain for the acceptance of the members of your Corporation. And I may explain that I purposely delayed giving Messrs. Bragg the commission for the execution of the ornament in question until I received from you the announcement that the newly-elected Corporation were willing to accept this token of my individual congratulation and goodwill towards yourself and them. Begging again to assure you and your community generally of my best wishes for many happy new years.

"I remain, my dear Mr. Mayor,
"Your most faithful servant,
DARTMOUTH

Reuben Farley, Esq.
"The Mayor of West Bromwich."

It was recorded that at the same Council Meeting the Mayor presented the Corporation with a Silver Mace. After thanking the Mayor for his valuable gift to the Town, the following letter was read:

Illuminated Page, to commemorate Alderman Reuben Farley's election as the first Mayor of West Bromwich.

"Town Hall, West Bromwich, 19th December, 1882.

"Dear Mr. Mayor,
"On behalf of the Officers of the Corporation, I beg to offer to present to you and the Corporation, a Mayoral Robe and Hat, for the use of the Mayor of this Borough, to mark our appreciation of the valuable services rendered by you to the Town as Chairman of the Improvement Commissioners, and also as an expression of our good wishes for the Corporation in the future, and we trust that the good feeling which has previously existed between us may long continue.

"I am, dear Sir,
"Yours faithfully,
"JOHN T. EAYRS,
"Borough Surveyor."

The Mayoral Chain presented by the Earl of Dartmouth 1882

'The Mayoral chain is of 18-carat gold, and hallmarked. The larger links are arranged with oval medallions on shields of an Elizabethan character, and upon these are hereafter to be enamelled the arms or monograms of successive Mayors. These are surmounted by the civic crown, and between each larger link is a Stafford knot, which, as a cognisance of the Stafford family, and as an emblem of the county, has a double connection with West Bromwich. The chain curves towards the centre with a pair of maces, similar to the one described below, and in the midst are placed the armorial bearings of the Earl of Dartmouth, Lord of the Manor of West Bromwich. These are emblazoned in proper colours, and from them depend the arms of the borough itself, on a large badge oviform, with a rich Elizabethan border. (description of arms) The arms are beautifully carried out beneath, in an oval medallion, and below is the motto, enamelled in gold,' "*Labor omnia vincit*"

The Silver Mace presented by The Mayor, Alderman Reuben Farley 1882

"The mace is of a distinctive character, of full size, and worthy to take its place with that of any other of the older boroughs in the kingdom. The coronet border is decorated with mullets and fleur-de-lis, as is also the border which surrounds the shield of the borough arms. The vase portion of the head is decorated with the arms, crest and motto of the borough; and on the reverse a shield bearing an inscription recording the gift. The lower divisions are decorated at intervals with appropriate emblems, among which is the crest of the donor, and in very distinct words on an important border, "The Mace of the Borough of West Bromwich."

John M Day, former Town Clerk, said that,

'The Mayor's Chain of Office was quite heavy to wear. It had a detachable badge which formed a type of pendant, which could be worn with a ribbon for less formal occasions. West Bromwich had a well understood protocol as to the wearing of the Regalia. The full rig was reserved for very formal occasions e.g. the Annual Meeting of the Council; receiving VIPs; Mayors Sunday and the like. The robe and chain were worn at Monthly Council meetings at which the Town Clerk was also robed. The Armistice Ceremony in Dartmouth Park would qualify for the full rig and the Evening Display and Service in the Town Hall.

On less formal occasions, the chain would be worn without the robe. Visits to Industry and the like would use just the badge. The Mace is the symbol of the Mayor's authority and, on formal occasions, is carried by the Mayor's Sargeant or Mace Bearer who precedes the Mayor.

When the Mayor visited other Boroughs, a different protocol was used. The chain would not be worn without the approval of the Mayor of that Borough. Consent was usually forthcoming, but the protocol had to be followed.'

The Mayor

A Meeting of the Town Council (being the First Meeting, and also the First Quarterly Meeting) was held in the Council Chamber, West Bromwich Town Hall on Thursday, the 9 day of November, 1882. At this historic meeting the Charter of Incorporation was entered in the Minutes and Councillor Reuben Farley was unanimously elected as first Mayor of the Municipal Borough of West Bromwich *(Minutes)*. In 1896 he was honoured by being the first person to be awarded the Freedom of the Borough.

The right to appoint a Mayor derived from the Royal Charter of Incorporation granted in 1882, when the 'Borough of West Bromwich' was constituted. Portraits of all the Mayors of West Bromwich are displayed on the walls in Room A in the Town Hall. It would be too great a task to list the merits and achievements of all these worthy First Citizens of the town, for this would require a publication of its own, but their names live on through various institutions, public works, and trust funds not to mention street names and parks.

A new Mayor was elected each year at the Annual Council Meeting, held in the Town Hall in the month of May, although the criteria for selection appears to have changed with the passing years.

Mayor Making in the Borough of West Bromwich at the Annual Council meetings as recalled by Joshua Churchman JP, first Mayor of the enlarged Borough of West Bromwich 1966-1967.

'The retiring Mayor, minus the Mayoral Robe, takes the Chair of the Meeting. Meanwhile, the person awaiting election is taken to the Artist's room at the rear of the stage, the purpose of this is that, should the nomination be controversial they would be unaware of it.

The incoming Mayor's proposer and seconder then address the meeting giving some background to the person they are sponsoring. Then they go to the Artist's Room to escort the proposed Mayor into the Council Meeting.

At this point the retiring Mayor calls for a vote to be taken by a show of hands, for the election of the new Mayor. This having been determined, he is dressed by the Mayor's Sergeant in the Robe and Chain of Office.

The Mayor and Mayoress, Mr and Mrs Joshua Churchman, greeting guests at the Mayor's Ball. With kind permission of Joshua Churchman.

Before taking over the Chair of the Meeting he is requested by the Town Clerk to declare his acceptance of the Office of Mayor and signs the declaration. Following this, he places the Badge of Office on the Deputy Mayor and Mayoress. It is then customary for the Mayor to address the assembly.'

Mayor's Appointments by John M Day

'The Official Visitors Book was kept in the Parlour, but at some stage, it was decided to provide a second book to become the Mayor's property at the end of his or her Mayoral Year. Visitors were accordingly invited to sign in both books. It was the custom for the Mayor's Secretary to maintain a scrapbook for each Mayor. This would comprise of press cuttings and invitations; programmes; photographs etc. This book would serve as a useful reminder for the Mayor to look back on.'

Sam Chiles recalls attending a Mayor Making Ceremony whilst working in the Town Hall,

'The Mayor Making Ceremony used to be held in the Town Hall. The first one I went to was when I was working in the Borough Treasurer's Office. We never thought of the Staff going because we were working. Mr Tommy Cotterill was the Mayor and Grace Cotterill became the next Mayor and she laid it down that the Staff should be allowed to come and have tea with them in the afternoon, in the Town Hall; so, if you wanted to go, you could. I remember going in, having a free cup of tea then you met the Mayor and Mayoress. The Town Clerk was dressed in his wig and there might be an MP there. You all shook hands as you went in. Mrs Cotterill insisted that the staff had the same privileges as everyone else.'

George Taylor recalls these reminiscences of that era when the Town Hall was still the venue for the induction of the new Mayor.

'Looking back at the start of my employment with the Council (1970s) I can remember working for several Mayors and Mayoresses at functions such as the Mayor's Charity Concerts and Mayor making nights. The whole of the stage and seats in front of the organ were decked with flowers, shrubs etc. The scent filled the whole of the Town Hall. The majority of the flowers and plants were grown by fellow workmen and women from Wigmore Nurseries. It is such a pity that the nurseries were closed and the majority of staff lost to private enterprise. The Mayor making ceremonies continued to be held at the Town Hall, until the new Civic centre was built in Oldbury in the early nineties. There are now no floral displays of the kind I have mentioned, possibly due to cost.'

CHAPTER 6
THE SURPRISE GIFT

The magnificent organ that dominates the stage in the Town Hall was the generous gift of Alexander Brogden, MP, in 1878. This musical gift was so unexpected that the rear of the Town Hall had to be altered and enlarged before the organ could be built. The *West Bromwich Weekly News* of 21 August 1875, *'Man About Town'* columnist recorded that:

> 'Mr Brogden's munificence has become a household word in the borough. He has substantially acknowledged the musical aspirations of the Town by the presentation of an organ, to be shortly placed in the Town Hall. The gift seemed to be as unexpected as it is generous for no suitable provision has been made for the 'King of instruments,' and I understand that a recess at the rear of the hall will have to be altered before the organ can be built.'

It is difficult for non-musicians to appreciate fully the importance of this particular organ, although no one would underestimate the value of this musical instrument in the life of the community. There is no doubt that in the early days, and indeed during the passing years, this instrument has played a significant role in the religious and secular life of the population.

To do justice to this 'jewel in our crown' it is necessary to gain information about it, in the first instance, from official sources provided by the local archives, which is as follows:

> 'This is one the finest organs of its type in the country. It was built by Forster and Andrews of Hull following the International Exhibition of 1862 and is one of twelve built for Town Halls up and down the country by that firm.
>
> At the opening ceremony for the Town Hall in 1875 Alexander Brogden, MP, promised to pay for a new organ for the hall. On 11 May 1878 flags were flown on the Town Hall to celebrate the opening of the Grand Organ.
>
> The organ has been extremely lucky to have survived the "vandalism" which has over taken many such organs and we are still able to hear the instrument largely as it was originally built.
>
> The tone of the organ is very similar to the work of Herr Edmund Schulze, a German organ builder of the day, who because of unexpected illness recommended Forster and Andrews to carry out his contracted work in

England. During the years 1862-1870 the flue voicer Herr Vogel, who was employed by Schulze, came to England and joined Forster and Andrews, hence the Germanic influence so evident in the West Bromwich organ sound.

The sound of the organ is very dependant first of all upon the metal used in the manufacture of the pipes and secondly on the scale and diameter of their voicing.

In 1953 the organ was completely stripped and cleaned at a cost of £534.

In 1984, Nicholson's, organ builders of Malvern, undertook and meticulously restored this fine example of a Victorian organ including the original actions to their former condition.'

Organ Specification

Manual Compass, CC to C ....61 notes
Pedal Compass, CCC to F ....30 notes
Great Organ consists of some 793 pipes ranging from 2ft to 16ft
Swell Organ consists of some 842 pipes ranging from 2ft to 16ft
Solo/Echo Organ consists of some 404 pipes ranging from 2ft to 8ft
Pedal Organ consists of some 180 pipes ranging from 8ft to 16ft (*Plate V i*)

Dr Roland Rogers, a native of West Bromwich and former organist at Bangor Cathedral, gave the first organ recital on 6 May 1878. Two days later Mr W William Hartland was appointed Borough Organist and remained until 1912. (*Midland Chronicle 1978*)

West Bromwich Borough Organists.

Mr William Hartland   (1878-1912)
Mr George W Shephard   (1912-1937)
Mr William (Bill) T Good   (1937-1974)

George W Shephard, Borough Organist, by G Shephard Johns

'My grandfather G W Shephard was Borough Organist at West Bromwich from 1912 to 1937 when he retired. He gave regular 'free' recitals and established the annual carol service tradition.

He was conductor and accompanist of the West Bromwich Choral Society for forty-four years which gave regular Concerts in the Town hall. Both my mother and grandmother were singers in the Society in the early 1900's period. My mother died in 1940 aged 46 years and grandmother died in 1935 aged 62 years. My grandfather died in 1962 aged 91 years.

My grandfather supervised the teaching of music in the junior schools in the Borough and visited each school during the year to give advice.

The school choirs sang in concerts at the Town Hall and I recall that when I was in the Choir my grandfather would, when coming down from the organ console to the front of the stage to conduct the choir, pat me on the head and say, "One day you will play this organ." I never did I'm afraid but I did sit on the organ stool sometimes when he was playing.

My grandfather's dressing room was off the curved corridor under the stage and he kept his music rostrum here and a bust of Beethoven. He met Edward Elgar on several occasions and conducted a section of the City of Birmingham Symphony Orchestra when they performed at the West Bromwich Town Hall.

A notice-board giving details of recitals and concerts was on the left hand side of the main entrance, and programmes for these events were one penny each.

The Town Hall was used for other events of course such as Political Party Conferences and meetings and he would be asked to play at some of these events.

The Town Hall Organ was his pride and joy and he would go up to practice during the week for the following Sunday's recital. He had two pianos at home and gave pianoforte lessons. One piano had two keyboards and pedals to simulate an organ. The other piano was a Broadwood concert grand.

Brass band concerts were given in Dartmouth Park and my grandfather

George W Shephard, Borough Organist, West Bromwich, 1912 – 1937. With kind permission of George S Johns.

George Shephard Johns, grandson of George W Shephard.

used to conduct on occasions. His father was the conductor of a band at Golds Hill and I have a silver whistle which was presented to him in1883. So music seems to run in the family.'

Ken Sower, who now lives in Shropshire, wrote the following amusing account:

Reminiscences of a Town Hall Concert by Ken Sower

'I was born in 1923, a fact for which I can not personally vouch, as I have no recollection of the event. However, the details are well documented, so that I can record them with some confidence. It took place in Sam's Lane, but my parents moved almost at once to a house they had been building in the Beeches Road area, so that it was Beeches Road Infants School that I first timorously entered in 1928. That I do remember, as I also recall a visit to the school by a Mr Shephard, then Borough Organist and Director of Music, who was seeking singing talent to make up a schools Choir to perform a public concert in the Town Hall. I had a good singing voice, and so became one of the chosen few who duly appeared before a real live playing audience.

Whether the entrance fee charged was considered worth while I cannot record. My parents, under fierce cross-examination, were polite but non-committal. We sang Handel's "*Where ere you walk*", and both score and lyrics stay with me to this day. My singing voice earned me more recognition in later life, but that is another story.'

Sam Chiles recalled that when they installed the electric blower for the organ, in the curved corridor around the back of the organ, there was a cupboard with a big door and the controls to the organ were behind that door. "You had to switch on before you played to provide the air and all that."

Audrey Burton, a retired Primary School teacher from West Bromwich, whose family were life-long friends of Borough Organist, William T Good, has very fond memories of many enjoyable evenings spent at concerts in the Town Hall and she recalls many of the highlights for us, as follows:

The Organ in the 1960s by Audrey Burton

'Mr Kirby from Walsall used to tune that organ. My lad, before they had humidity control, used to help him and take two or three friends and they would have a bucket chain, particularly when the weather was dry and very hot. They had to keep about ten buckets of water in the organ. If you can imagine them trundling up all those steps to open the doors at the side to put all these buckets of water to stand. There was a door that went in at the back of the organ and they were refilled about twice a year.

I know my lads used to go with about five or six friends so that one could be filling the bucket because the kitchen is the other side of the corridor, or it was then, to bring it to the first stop. There were three platforms and five steps, then a three. They would give them to Mr Good, who was the last one by the organ, and he would put them where he wanted them. It was usually during the summer months. They were galvanised buckets so it was quite a job to get them up the steps and stages to the organ.

Gas Lights

I remember they had mottled bowls and a chain to pull them on if there was an electricity cut. One Sunday Festival night they had a terrific storm. It just came from nowhere at the end of October. The lights went out in the 60s and these gas lights were a godsend because there were about eighty children on the platform. The conductor shouted, "Stand still!" because the children wanted to run to their moms in the audience but it was all right because these lights came on and it was resumed ten minutes later.

1963 Children's Sunday School Concert. With kind permission of Audrey Burton.

W T Good arranged Organ Recitals on Sunday evenings between September and March at fortnightly intervals. He invited various soloists to sing or play an instrument, sometimes school choirs or mixed choirs participated in these Recitals.'

Choral Society Concerts

'The Choral Society had a committee comprising of a Chairman, Treasurer, Social Secretary and a Committee usually selected from Choral Members.

Mrs Ada Jones was the Choral Society Secretary for many, many years and she lived in Hill House, Dagger Lane, West Bromwich.

Concerts took place in March or April and September or October, when the choral works were performed and professional artists sang the solos. Sometimes an orchestra accompanied them, otherwise the piano or organ was used.

W T Good became Borough Organist in 1937 and held that position until 1974. During this time Ezra Bagnall was the pianist or organist to many of these concerts. Ezra Bagnall faithfully played voluntarily to most of the rehearsals and performances. W T Good was the conductor and sometimes his wife Lucy sang soprano solos. Ezra Bagnall was organist and choir master at All Saints' Church and later Holy Trinity Church.

At some Choral Society Concerts - *Messiah* or *Elijah* or *Judas Maccabaeus* were performed. *Brigadoon* and many other works were performed.

At this time it was quite a social commitment as friends frequently invited other singers to go to their church and help with a production that was being performed. Many friendships were formed in this way. At this time the Choral Society was about 120 strong comprising Soprano, Alto, Tenor and Bass.

At some miscellaneous concerts favourite arias were sung or a guest instrumentalist was invited, for example, Max Jaffa (Palm Court of Grand Hotel) and Ezra Bagnall accompanied him. Everyone was delighted. On another occasion opera singer and Bass Baritone, Owen

William T Good, Borough Organist, West Bromwich, 1937-1974 Courtesy of Audrey Burton.

Brannigan sang his famous, *Mud, Mud, Glorious Mud!* Anne Ziegler and Webster Booth also performed at another concert and delighted their audience. Jan Berenzka and his orchestra played at another concert. His cornet player played a solo (He was named Jack Boffy). My family knew this person. The Kenrick & Jefferson Male Voice Choir and the Coseley Male Voice Choir sang at some Saturday or Sunday evening concerts. Evelyn Grees had a delightful Ladies Choir and they sang at the Town Hall on many occasions.

My parents (Mr & Mrs E Dunn) were members for many years, so was I and later my youngest son Christopher Loach met his future wife Christine in 1970 at a Choral Society rehearsal and they married in 1974.

During the early seventies we had lots of electricity cuts and this stopped many members from attending in the evening as many members were getting old, interest seemed to wane and the committee decided to disband the weekly practices. The only time members came was to help at the Remembrance Services and Carol Concerts.

W T Good ceased to be Borough Organist in 1974 but still continued to play for the Remembrance and Carol Services.'

Despite the terrific amount of time, energy, enthusiasm and dedication displayed by these Borough organists, it appears that at times they felt a little despondent about the results of their labours. Frank Burton, Audrey's husband, repeated a conversation he had with his friend, William (Bill) T Good, the Borough Organist.

He said, "Nobody really appreciates music"

I said, "It's true you don't, but there's one thing that certain about it."

He said, "What's that?"

I replied, "You think that you are not remembered and all the rest of it. Well, I'll tell you what. People will still be remembering your music when they've long forgotten my job here!"

He said, "You know, I never thought of that!"

Mr Burton said, "They didn't you know! They never realised what they were giving. It was just there and they gave it and it was fantastic!"

Carol Sunday

'This Carol Service took place between 17-22 December. These were wonderful Services, various artists took part and every seat was taken in the hall. Mr Jefferson Cottrell or a member of his family chaired the proceedings.

Programmes for this occasion were donated by Kenrick & Jefferson. W T Good was organist and Choir Master at Queen Street Methodist Church for thirty-one years.'

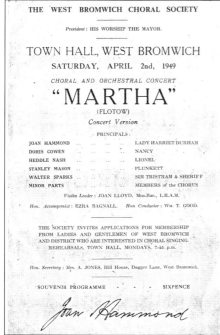

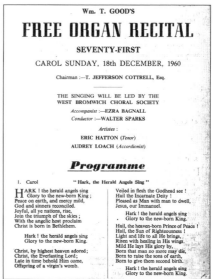

Clockwise from top left: 1912: Free Organ Recital Programme by W Hartland. With kind permission of George S Johns. 1937: Free Organ Recital Programme by G W Shephard. With kind permission of George S Johns. 1949: The West Bromwich Choral Society Programme for the Opera "MARTHA" With kind permission of Leslie Lofthouse. 1960: Free Organ Recital Carol Service. With kind permission of Audrey Burton.

Sunday School Festival by Audrey Burton

'This Annual Sunday School Festival was held on Friday to Saturday in October. Children from Sunday Schools in the Borough received prizes for attendance during the year and often sang solos or played their musical instrument.

Leslie Greenaway who was organist and choirmaster at St. Philip's Church conducted the choir and W T Good played the organ. This choir was augmented by many members from various churches. The Hall was full and the platform had approximately sixty to eighty children with the choir at the back of the platform to augment their singing. It was a wonderful sight and so pleasing to see so many parents participating and encouraging their children.'

Remembrance Sunday

'This was a very moving Service. The platform was filled by various organisations, Boys Brigade, St John Ambulance, Red Cross, Scouts, Girl Guides, Army Training Corps, Air Training Corps, and Sea Cadets.'

Reg Thompson supplied an amusing anecdote about the condition of the organ when Reginald Dixon, the well-known and accomplished organist, came to give a concert in the Town Hall. Reg takes up the story:

A Remembrance Service in the Main Hall.

Reginald Dixon's Concert by Reg Thompson

'The organ had to be refurbished. We moved all the big seats on the stage so that they could get to the organ base at the front and we moved the seats so that they could get to the doors. Two chappies came. There was a fellow and an apprentice and they stayed for six weeks. We helped them out on anything they'd got to have and we had to fetch it for them.

Then came the night when Reginald Dixon came to commission it. In the first half of his programme he groped around the organ because he hadn't got a clue. He couldn't play it to the standards he was capable of, but in the second half he knocked the hell out of it! But the laugh came afterwards when my brother and I went down to meet him. Bill Good was the organist and he said, "Come down and meet Mr Dixon."

So we went down and while we were talking to him this old lady came up and said,

"Mr Dixon?"

"Yes my love," he said, "What's the matter?"

She said, " I don't know why the Corporation spent money on having the organ refurbished because you could have done it the way you played in the second half and blown all the dust out!"'

It is interesting to note that in later years air conditioning was installed in the Town Hall, although this was not, apparently, so much for the comfort of the worthy citizens of the town, but for the purpose of providing the correct temperature and humidity for the wood and leather in the organ. Nowadays, its condition is maintained on a contract to ensure that there are no problems.

On a more serious note Sandwell Metropolitan Borough Council organises a Free Organ Recital once a month in the Town Hall and invites distinguished organists to play mainly

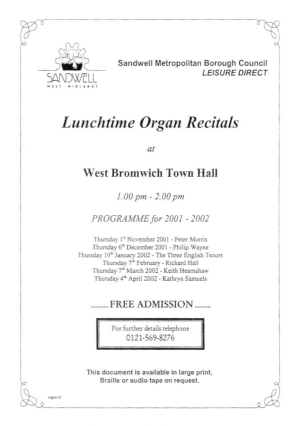

Sandwell Metropolitan Borough Council
LEISURE DIRECT

SANDWELL
WEST MIDLANDS

Lunchtime Organ Recitals

at

West Bromwich Town Hall

1.00 pm - 2.00 pm

PROGRAMME for 2001 - 2002

Thursday 1st November 2001 - Peter Morris
Thursday 6th December 2001 - Philip Wayne
Thursday 10th January 2002 - The Three English Tenors
Thursday 7th February - Richard Hall
Thursday 7th March 2002 - Keith Hearnshaw
Thursday 4th April 2002 - Kathryn Samuels

.... FREE ADMISSION ....

For further details telephone
0121-569-8276

This document is available in large print,
Braille or audio tape on request.

Lunchtime Organ Recital Programme 2001-2002. Courtesy of SMBC, Leisure Direct.

popular and light-classical music. 'Now in their fifteenth successive year these popular, free recitals have at times attracted audiences of over 200 from all walks of life, old and young.' *(SMBC Leisure Direct)*

The popular and versatile organist Nigel Ogden, the presenter of the BBC Radio Two's *The Organist Entertains,* gave a lunch time concert at the Town Hall, 8 February 2001, which was well attended by an appreciative audience which included the grandson of George W Shephard, a former West Bromwich Borough Organist.

Guest organist, Nigel Ogden, pictured at the Town Hall's organ, 2001.
With kind permission of Nigel Ogden.

CHAPTER 7

THE BASTION OF THE TOWN'S DEFENCES (1939 – 1945)

*"What went on in the Town Hall during the war
was always a mystery to most people." (Anon)*

The following reminiscences may shed some light upon the part played by West Bromwich Town Hall during World War II and how it was elected to be the "bastion" of defence for the afflicted wartime population of the town. The basement of the building was designated as the focal point of the Borough's protection and defences against the aggressors. Prior to responding to this clarion call to arms, the area was used to deposit dusty, long forgotten archives which recorded the history of the town's glorious past. At that time the basement's only token towards the defence of the town appeared to be several somewhat daunting large cellars, heavily protected with strong iron-barred doors, previously used to house "prisoners" awaiting to hear their fate in the Magistrates Court a flight of stone steps leading into a brick wall being the only evidence of this little bit of history. However, things were set to change dramatically in that basement and cellars, just as they were in all other areas of life.

The various accounts related here rely heavily upon the experiences of the personnel who worked in the Town Hall during the war and people who were associated with the Borough or different voluntary organisations.

Once more we rely upon our first-hand accounts of the town's preparation for the war with these memories of Sam Chiles.

'One thing about the Town Hall, when they said there might be a war, the Corporation decided to organise volunteers course and they decided that the basement of the Town Hall should be the Air Raid Precautions (ARP) Headquarters in case of any bombs.

So, they employed a constructional firm out of Bagnall Street, Golds Hill to convert the basement into an Air Raid Precautions Control Centre. They sunk girders into the concrete all the way down that basement and across the top they put very strong corrugated steel sheets, right across to make a tunnel of it. They didn't use the Strong Room, they had the Borough Surveyors and Town Clerk's Rooms and our strong rooms on that side where they kept the documents etc. There were three rooms on this side where they kept the documents and rubbish and things. So, they cleared those out.

One room they made into a telephone exchange and the bigger one they made into a map room. There were big maps on the wall, red stuff for fire, blue for high explosives and gold for gas.

Of course I was working, I used to be cashier by then, and I used to go down there every night to lock the money up in the strong room and fetch it out every morning so course I could see the progress they were making, but on the first raid they had in West Bromwich they dropped a bomb on the laundry in Edward Street and this put all the telephones out of action. Some of the girls from the office used to go to work on the switchboard in the basement. That was when that young girl, Charity Bick, got that George Medal for her bravery during the Blitz.

Jim Hayes, retired Mayor's chauffeur, mentioned the existence of an old bicycle which is still stored in the Town Hall basement. When the bicycle was pedalled furiously, it was intended to activate a generator to provide electricity for use in an emergency during the war. In the same area of the basement, the relic of a switchboard is pushed on one side to accommodate the pipes of the central heating system. In this day and age of sophisticated satellite communications that switchboard looks antiquated and totally inadequate for any but the most basic means of communication and yet, it probably had its moment of glory, and retains a place in the history of the town.

The Civil Defence
John M Day explains the role of the Civil Defence Service

'The Town Clerk, Mr G F Darlow was appointed as Civil Defence Controller. I was one of his Deputies.

A full time Civil Defence Officer was appointed before war was declared. He was involved in recruitment and training of the several hundred volunteers for the various branches of the Service, i.e. Rescue, First Aid, Ambulances, Wardens and Headquarters Staff.

Fortunately, shortly before the War, West Bromwich purchased premises in the Town Centre, fronting Pitt Street and these premises became part of the Civil Defence Offices with a large room to the rear of Pitt Street and it was used for other Civil Defence Services.

West Bromwich had already 'adopted' the Cruiser, HMS *Bermuda*, and the Civil Defence Services adopted HM Submarine *Trespasser*.'

Reg Thompson, who worked for West Bromwich Corporation, once more sets the scene and informs us of the changes made to the basement of the Town Hall in preparation for it to become the nerve-centre of communications.

'I went to the Corporation and got a job. There were quite a lot of us preparing the basement for the ARP room. The basement ceiling was reinforced with iron beams and we cleared out the rooms which they used to put the records in. We cleared them all out and converted them into the control room and the other rooms were for the fellow in charge and the deputy, bedrooms and what have you. There was a signalling system built by Mr Brookes, the pathologist from Hallam Hospital. He put it in the top of the tower and he signalled to everyone in the area what was going on.

At that time Hallam Hospital belonged to the Corporation and we had a workshop and you could guarantee that every morning when we were having breakfast and he was covered in blood he would come and hand his cigarettes round. Oh, he was a devil but a very, very brainy man, but the work he did could have cost the Corporation hundreds of pounds in those days.

We erected a lift in the Town Hall spire, where you open the window, catch a rope, go down the rope and find yourself on the ground, 130ft down! That was the emergency exit for the people who were on duty, just in case anything happened.

The ARP room hadn't been working very long when our dear friend dropped a bomb. As soon as the first bomb was dropped and it dropped by the library, it put everything out of commission. We were on ARP at the time and we tried to get into the Town Hall and we couldn't, so my friend, Jack Parker, said "I'll go." And so he went. He was away quite a while and we found out later that he was on the edge of a bomb crater in Lombard Street. He was on the edge of that crater and when he came back he was shaking like a leaf. (1940)'

An anonymous contributor made the following observations.

'In 1939, when the war was imminent, a mountain of sandbags was erected outside the entrance to the Town Hall, I think this may have been due to the large plate glass windows on each side of the main steps. What went on in the Town Hall during the war was always a mystery to most people, but it was suggested it was the centre for Civil Defence and responsible for Air Raid Precautions and Invasions. But the bills still had to be paid and the Rates and Council rents seemed to be paid at the Town Hall in those times.'

The staff in the Borough Treasurer's Department did more than their fair share to help win the war according to these memories narrated by Sam Chiles. Perhaps it is pertinent to inform everyone that Sam served during the Second World War in the Royal Canadian Air Force, 428 Squadron, which was based in York from 1944 to 1945. He was awarded a Distinguished Flying Cross for bravery and courage by King George VI in 1946.

The Volunteer Services by Sam Chiles

The Auxiliary Fire Service (AFS) and The Air Raid Precautions (ARP)

'Twelve months before the war started, after Chamberlain and Hitler signed that agreement at Munich, the government realised that there was a possibility of war and they started up the ARP (Air Raid Precautions).

One day I was on the cash counter taking the money for the gas, rates, electricity etc. when two drivers came into the Town Hall yard with a big van and they carried hundreds and hundreds of parcels. They'd got nowhere to put them and they stacked them under the clock opposite my counter.

I said, "What is that?"

They said, "Oh, it's ARP. You have to volunteer and these are the forms." So, when I locked up and had locked the money down in the strong room, I thought I would have a look and see what they were all about and so I opened a few. I opened one and they were pink forms as I remember, 'Auxiliary Fire Service', so I joined that! I took a form out, went home, filled it in, went to Dr. Gordon, got examined (he charged me half-a-crown) took it back to the office and sent it down to the Fire Station.

A bit later on in the day I was phoned by the Chief Fire Officer.

"This form you've sent round here," he said, "What is it all about?" He was the Chief Fire Officer and he didn't know that he'd got to form an auxiliary fire service. So I know from that form that I was the first volunteer in the AFS. I trained under Arthur Wash for four nights a week in fire-fighting and anti-gas drill. We had a written exam and so on – I qualified!

When the war was declared I was called out from the office on the Friday morning. I was on call you see and in an emergency I was called out. I had to tell the Treasurer. He wasn't very pleased but he couldn't do anything about it, so I got a Corporation driver, a lorry and a pump trailing on the back and I opened the Fire Station in the indoor Market Place at the corner of Slater Street, Great Bridge.

We couldn't have any lights on, hadn't got any water and had to sweep the place up. We hadn't got an office and we couldn't have any lights on because it had a glass roof which hadn't been blacked out. So, I built an office with two market stalls and blacking out paper and pinned it round all over. We hadn't got a phone so at night we had to sit two blokes in the fish shop. We put two blokes in case one fell asleep waiting for the phone to ring, so that was the AFS. I was there nearly every night for twelve months from about seven o'clock at night until seven o'clock in the morning. One morning they were appealing for air-gunners on the radio so three of us decided to volunteer.'

Ken Sower, in his reminiscences refers to the war years and this is his recollection of the Volunteer Services in West Bromwich.

The ARP (Air Raid Precautions) by Ken Sower

'In 1939 the Grammar School was evacuated to Tamworth, and returned in 1940. A few senior boys, including myself, who had volunteered for ARP duties and who lived within a reasonable distance, were appointed to the staff of the ARP Control Room. This was located in a specially reinforced underground room at the front of the Town Hall. I spent some time there during exercises and uneventful raids, until one memorable night when there was the first of several heavy raids. I arrived breathless at my post, only to find that almost the first bomb to have fallen had landed on the pavement immediately in front of the Town Hall, destroying the telephone cable, and so rendering the Control Room completely ineffective. I was asked to go out and help where I could and so I spent the next forty-eight hours with the Rescue Squads, disinterring bodies (some dead, some alive) out of the ruins of a badly bombed street somewhere behind the Town Hall.

After twenty-four hours sleep I returned to the task of recovering at least one more lady still amazingly alive. After a period of further raids with more education in-between, I joined the army and spent the years of 1943-46 in Egypt. In 1950 I married and moved to Wolverhampton, and made some friends at a new Town Hall. In particular the Chief Medical Officer of Health, a Dr Jim Galloway, who later filled the equivalent position in West Bromwich. He was a man of great charm and wit, and his loss was a source of deep regret. It ended my last link with West Bromwich Town Hall.'

There were many unsung heroes and heroines in the West Bromwich Volunteer Services during the war and, perhaps, only their families know of their acts of courage and

Miss Bick yesterday

Shy Charity, the heroine no-one knew

ONCE again fame will shine on shy war heroine Charity Bick.

For 22 years Charity, who at the age of 14 won the George Medal for courage during the Blitz, has lived in obscurity.

The medal, received from King George VI, has lain all that time in a cigar box. But now, after a long search, the lost heroine has been found. She will be the honoured guest next week when the Imperial War Museum in London launches a history magazine.

The first issue carries a picture of Charity in ARP uniform and steel helmet, taken from a painting by war artist A.R. Thomson.

She wears the medal she won the night she helped put out an incendiary bomb and then cycled through hails of shrapnel carrying despatches to the town hall in West Bromwich, West Midlands.

The museum had a hard job tracing Charity. Eventually she was found in Forres in the North of Scotland.

Miss Bick, now 63, said yesterday: 'I don't mind coming out of hiding for this.'

Brave Charity as she was painted

This newspaper article describes the courage of Charity Bick in the worst Blitz in West Bromwich during the Second World War. (Newspaper unknown)

bravery but recording these memories of long ago provides us with an opportunity to acknowledge, salute and express our gratitude to them.

There was, however, one young girl whose bravery is placed on record and well documented but it is worthy of a place in the history of the Town Hall as it relates to the failure in its communications system. This girl was anxious to play her part, as a despatch rider, in the Volunteer Services of her native town and by her acts of bravery she became a legend in her own lifetime.

Miss Charity Anne Bick was actually fourteen years old when she joined the Volunteer Services, but she persuaded her father to sign a declaration form stating that she was sixteen and therefore eligible for voluntary work. This fact alone shows a girl of spirit and great determination which was to carry her through one of the worst nights of bombing in the history of the town.

In November 1940, during the worst of the Blitz she cycled to the Town Hall carrying important despatches and helped her father to put out an incendiary fire in a shop. King George VI presented Charity Anne Bick with the George Medal for bravery. (*Plate IV iii*)

The West Bromwich Library User Group was thrilled to receive a letter from Charity Bick, from her home in Scotland. It reads as follows:

Dear User Group,

What a lovely surprise to receive a large envelope containing so many goodies. I have read your book and enjoyed renewing my acquaintance with so many places that I knew when I was growing up. Dartmouth Park was one of few places Mother allowed George (my brother) and I to go alone. We spent a lot of time on the swings and on the lake in a boat.

Would you please put this little cheque into your postal fund or something. Someone else can be as I was when they receive something from you.

Please excuse my 'shoogly' writing but since the lorry knocked me down last December my writing is all over the place. I've had to abandon my Fountain pen as it made my writing look as though a drunken spider had wandered across the page!

Thank you again, so very much,
Sincerely,
Charity Bick.

It is quite evident that Charity had not lost her sense of humour nor that indomitable spirit which saw her through much adversity during the war with her spell as a Volunteer Depatch Rider.

(i) Town Hall, main corridor, with its 'encaustic tiled pavement' leading to a stone stairway to the gallery. The doors into the main hall are opposite the EXIT sign to the High Street.

(ii) Stained glass window, main stairway, with a crest of a blast furnace and two kilns either side encircled by the motto, "Labor Omnia Vincit" with the Staffffordshire Knot underneath.

(iii) Stained glass window, with the Coat of Arms in the door panel of the main corridor.

(iv) Stained glass window, either side of the stage in the main hall.

(i) Maw & Co encaustic tile pavements are laid along the three corridor floors in the Town Hall.

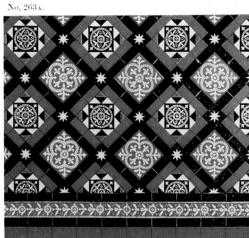

(ii) Examples of Maw & Co floor tiles, from an original pattern tile catalogue in the collection of the Ironbridge Gorge Museum. Courtesy of Ironbridge Gorge Museum Trust, Shropshire.

(i) The West Bromwich County Borough Coat of Arms in the Council Chamber.

(ii) Charter of the Grant of Arms. This is the original Charter of the Grant of Arms made to the Borough of West Bromwich in 1882. This original charter was removed and replaced with a copy in April 2002.

(iii) A copper plaque situated above the doors leading into the main hall is engraved with a list of names of the town's fallen heroes who served in the Boer War (1899 - 1902).

(i) West Bromwich's Coat of Arms.

(ii) The Mayoral Chair with a carving similar to the crest in the stained glass window.

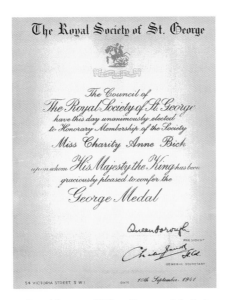

(iii) Certificate of The George Medal Awarded to Charity Anne Bick, 10 September 1941. Courtesy of Lyng Primary School Archives.

(iv) HMS BERMUDA Badge in the main corridor, contains the following inscription: Presented by the Lords Commissioners of the Admiralty to West Bromwich to commemorate the town's adoption of HMS Bermuda.

(i) The main hall with a view of the stage and organ.

(ii) Sandwell Youth Music, Junior Strings Orchestra in West Bromwich Town Hall. With kind permission of Sandwell Music.

(i) Doreen Mary Young (nee Smith) playing the piano in the Town Hall on a nostalgic return visit to West Bromwich during October 2001. 'Dorrie' was a pupil and pianist for the then Cronehills Girl's School from 1933 to 1937. Also, she played the full grand piano for the St John's Church May Festival, each year in West Bromwich Town Hall. With kind permission of Doreen M Young.

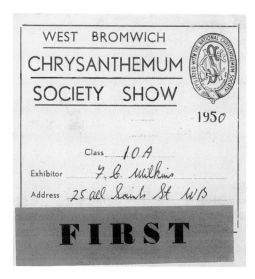

(ii) West Bromwich Chrysanthemum Society Show. A Certificate awarded to Francis Charles Wilkins, 1950. Other certificates awarded were as follows:

1948 - Class 3a: Second, No date - Class 5a: Second
1950 - Class 3a: First, 1950 - Class 6a: Third

Classification of Chrysanthemums,
by The National Chrysanthemum Society:
Class 3a: Indoor Curved, large flowered.
Class 5a: Indoor Intermediate, large flowered.
Class 6a: Indoor Anemone, large flowered.
Class 10a: Indoor Spider Chrysanthemum.
(The Royal Horticultural Society)

From the author's collection.

(i) Sandwell Youth Music, Junior and Intermediate Brass Bands, West Bromwich Town Hall. With kind permission of Sandwell Music.

(ii) West Bromwich Library User Group, 2002. Photo taken on the main stairway, in front of the stained glass window in West Bromwich Town Hall. Members names are as follows, starting at the top of the stairway: Keith Kilvert, Fred Barnfield, Anne Wilkins, Derrick de Faye, Doreen Shakespeare, Jim Shakespeare, Robin Pearson.

Anne Wilkins, West Bromwich Library User Group.
With kind permission of the Express & Star, Wolverhampton 2002.

CHAPTER 8
THE TOWN HALL AND THE NAVY

'Once Navy, Always Navy'

It seems strange that a town as landlocked as West Bromwich, so far from the sea, should have contact with the Navy but it is a fact that the population of the town was involved and had an interest in the ships and their crews during those traumatic war-time years. It comes as no surprise to the townspeople who experienced the rigours of war and wartime shortages that the National Warship Campaign Week should have been so well supported, for everyone had some commitment to the war effort whether it involved land or sea.

It may not be general knowledge that the first ship adopted by the town was the HMS *Galatea*. A local paper, *The Midland Chronicle & Free Press* printed the following, poignant story regarding the West Bromwich, 'Warship Campaign Week'.

'One of the many touching incidents during Warship Week was provided by an old lady living in the South of England who wrote enclosing a five-shilling Postal Order to help our Warship Week and a letter saying that she was married at St. Peter's Church, West Bromwich, forty years ago and has a son serving on HMS *Galatea*.' (*source: "Gossip of the Week" column by the Throstle*, December, 1941)

John M Day provided his own wartime memories:

'I do not know when West Bromwich 'adopted' the *Galatea*. I imagine it would have been very early in 1939 – 1945 War. The object was to befriend members of the crew with letters and comforts e.g. knitted articles provided by the Ladies' groups. Sadly the *Galatea* was sunk through enemy action. There were many casualties. This must have happened in the period 1940/41.

The Mayor opened an appeal for dependants. My only experience of the *Galatea* was when the appeal wound up. Difficulties arose about fund distribution and reference was needed to the Charity Commission for advice. I remember being involved in the legal work to sort things out.'

The following information is by courtesy of The Imperial War Museum, London.

HMS *Galatea*

'The light cruiser HMS *Galatea* was part of 15th Cruiser Squadron in December 1941. On the night of the 14th the Squadron was returning to Alexandria from an unsuccessful search for an enemy convey when it was attacked by German dive-bombers. The attacks persisted for seven hours. Just before midnight *Galatea* became a target for U 557 which hit her with two torpedoes in quick succession. The cruiser turned over and sank in three minutes. Captain Sim, 22 officers and 447 ratings were killed. About 100 survivors were picked up by the destroyers HMS *Griffin* and HMS *Hotspur*. HMS *Galatea* had seen much war service as she had taken part in the Norwegian campaign and the evacuation of the British Army from France in May-June 1940. She had also taken part in the rounding up of the *Bismark*.'

HMS *Bermuda*

The badge of *Bermuda* (*Plate IV iv*) has been displayed in the main corridor of West Bromwich Town Hall for many years and yet few people are aware of its history, except for the fact that it was 'adopted' by the town during the war. The badge for HMS *Bermuda* has, a demi-lion affronte erased red holding in the dexter paw a trident also red on a white background, is based on the arms of Bermuda. The Island of Bermuda's flag has the same creature in the same colour.

It is due to John M Day that details emerged which helped in the search for the history of the Bermuda and the town's connection with its crew. He writes:

'The town then "adopted" *Bermuda*, a Cruiser. Happily she survived the conflict and remained in service for some years afterwards. I think that the *Bermuda* was put into service around 1942. Two Civic visits were made to the ship. The first visit would have been in 1947. *Bermuda* was then at Chatham. Travelling by train we were met; escorted to our hotel and then taken on board, where we were entertained for the evening, with dinner aboard.

The 'Party' rejoined the ship the following morning for a conducted tour. This was preceded by a ceremony which has now been discontinued. I refer to the daily rum issue. This was conducted with formal procedure, which we were privileged to witness as the practise has since ceased.

The conducted tour was of great interest. I came away realising what magnificent ships our Navy possessed. After lunch aboard, the Civic Party returned by train to West Bromwich. We had learned how the ship's company appreciated the efforts of the West Bromwich ladies who had done so much for their comfort.

The second and last visit took place much later but I have not been able to pinpoint the dates! I think it may have been in the late 1950s or early 1960s.

The ship was approaching the end of her Service. She was then at Devonport. One thing did strike me however. Plymouth was still busy re-developing large areas devastated as a result of wartime bombing!

I had an idea that *Bermuda* was to be decommissioned. On reading in *The Times* that *Bermuda* was on her way to the breakers, I approached the Admiralty, enquiring if West Bromwich could be given the ship's bell, having regard to the long association of *Bermuda* with the Town.

The reply was to the effect that all naval ship's bells were offered for sale through public auction. There the matter rested.

However, several months later, the Town Hall Keeper rang through one morning, to say that a crate had been delivered addressed to the Town Clerk. My reaction was to ask, "What's in it?"

The Keepers reply was "I've no idea, but it's heavy."

We found, on opening the crate, that the Admiralty had sent the Bermuda Bell! The cost to the Borough was £8.18s.5d. for postage.

It was my idea that the Bell might be rung at the beginning and end of formal Council Meetings. This was agreed.

Before this however, a formal evening was organised, at which Members of the Council and Officers assembled together with the first Captain of *Bermuda*,

HMS Bermuda (C52) a 'Fiji' (Colony) Class Cruiser prepared for active service in 1942. With kind permission of the Royal Naval Association, West Bromwich.

and the last Captain and some members of the last crew. We had a great evening. The two Captains had never met! Subsequently the ship's bell was hung in the Council Chamber.

After Sandwell took over, the tradition was abandoned. The Bell was presented to the West Bromwich Royal Naval Association, where, I imagine, it is still at their Headquarters.'

The RNA motto, **Once Navy, Always Navy,** is no idle boast, as research into the *Bermuda* has revealed. A request on the Internet in the *Royal Naval Association's Monthly Circular*, London, for information from men who served on the ship brought forth the following reminiscences from former crew members. George Vernon, from Liverpool, served on the *Bermuda* in 1943 and states:

Arthur Wright, who served aboard HMS Bermuda from 1945-1946, is ringing the Bermuda Bell, which is in the safe hands of the Royal Naval Association, West Bromwich. With kind permission of Arthur Wright and the RNA, West Bromwich.

'In 1943 I, along with one thousand other men, went from Plymouth to Glasgow to John Brown's Shipyard to join a brand new ship. Everything was new, spoons, knives, forks all with HMS *Bermuda* on them. I don't know what happened to the cutlery but I think they were taken as souvenirs but I can't say anything about that.

Bermuda sailed to do trials out at sea as a Colony Class Cruiser. There was only a few of that Class. After about six weeks of going to sea and back to port we sailed to the British Home Fleet Base and up around the Islands in Scotland to await orders along with other Warships to patrol or escort Convoys to other places in the world i.e. Iceland, Russian convoys. She spent a lot of time around the Arctic on patrol. She was bombarded from the air a few times while on patrol.

HMS *Bermuda* left the Arctic cold to take part in the North Africa landings. She was chased by aircraft and missed being torpedoed. She done very well, not hit but she had some near misses, weaving in and out at full speed to miss them. She also went through the Suez Canal to Singapore via the Straits of Malacca; then came home to Plymouth after an eventful trip.

I left the ship to become a Leading Stoker and then on to be a Petty Officer. I spent five years in the Royal Navy and I am still in the Royal Naval Association, (RNA). I am eighty years old in a few weeks time.

HMS *Bermuda* was a good ship and did her bit in the War. She never made the headlines but she never got hit. She was a very lucky ship. After I left she went to Australia but then that was in peacetime but she made a name for herself.

I have got the Russian Medals and others and I still have a picture of *Bermuda*. I never knew that West Brom. had adopted her but it is nice to know. I have never ever been to your town or the Town Hall. I didn't know the RNA there had her Bell. The crest is, as you say, of the Island of Bermuda. I gave Liverpool RNA Club what I paid for; a wooden crest of the ship and it hangs up in Liverpool RNA.

I hope you like my story about HMS *Bermuda* – a good ship and nice to say when I was a lad of nineteen I served on her. I found it nice to tell you about HMS *Bermuda*.

Good luck and all the Best.'

(George Vernon, Liverpool, January, 2002)

Derek Holden, who still lives in West Bromwich, served on the *Bermuda* from 1943-1948, and made contact after reading an article in the *Express & Star*, dated 10 May 2002, about this research into HMS *Bermuda*. He provided the following information:

'I joined HMS *Bermuda* at Scapa Flow, roughly February 1943.

We saw service in the Far East as attached to the American 7th Fleet. During that time we patrolled the Pacific Islands keeping the Japanese in their island bases, until they decided to come out which was at Okinawa.

We were the first ship into Formosa which is now Taiwan. Our base was Australia and we were treated very well.

I can safely say there were only two West Bromwich sailors on board, myself and A/B Wilkins. We came back to Devonport in 1948 for de-commissioning.

Many years later, approximately in 1986, I had to catch a train in Manchester to come back to West Bromwich. I sat by a chap and his wife and started to chat to them. He asked if I had been in the Navy as he had served on HMS *Bermuda*. We discovered that, by a strange coincidence, I had taken his job over as a Radar Operator when I joined the ship in 1943.'
(A/B Seaman Holden, West Bromwich, June 2002)

Arthur Wright, Halesowen, served on HMS *Bermuda* from April 1945 and he wrote:

'I joined the *Bermuda* at Devonport (Guzz) in April 1945 after service on HMS *Active* 1943-1944 and HMS *Denbigh Castle* (sunk on Convoy to Russia's Kola Inlet), February 1945.

I was in the 'Asdic' Branch of the Royal Navy and was on Watch entering Formosa through the minefield. My main duties were 'Asdic Sweeper' and many 'Out of Bounds' Patrols.

'Mess 62 Hanger Deck' was where I was serving my time on board *Bermuda*.

As requested, I have provided a list of medals awarded:
1939-1945:   Star medals of France and Germany
                     Italian; Pacific; Atlantic Clasp; Victory medal
Russian Convoy: 2 Medals'
(W Arthur Wright (Shiner), Halesowen, September 2002)

Douglas Newell, Oxon, served on HMS *Bermuda* from 1946-1948 and wrote:

'It was very nice of you to put a piece in Headquarters Circular as this will be received by 149 branches of the RNA. I served on the *Bermuda* 1946-1948 and got rated to Petty Officer on her. On our arrival in Plymouth a representative on the Island of Bermuda came aboard to thank the crew. Everyone had a card from the people of Bermuda which entitled you to 200 cigarettes to take through the gate. We had two hundred at sixpence a packet of Senior Service.
(Douglas Newell, Oxon, February 2002)

Robert (Bob) Bolter, Birmingham, who served on HMS *Bermuda* from 1950–1953 wrote:

'The *Bermuda* was commissioned in September 1941. She was with ten others a Class of Cruisers all named after British Colonies at that time.

When these ships were built, Great Britain's War situation was very precarious and as a result armaments took precedence over living conditions; as a result that anyone serving on them as long as twenty years after the Second World War could relate to wartime conditions.

I served on the *Bermuda* during her two and a half-year commission as FlagShip of the South Atlantic Fleet based at Simonstown, South Africa 1950-1953. There were ratings serving aboard during that time that came from the Black Country and three I can remember from West Bromwich.

The Crest of HMS *Bermuda* is on the dry-dock wall (or was) at Simonstown, South Africa. It was painted by A/B Smith, 12 Mess For'wrd. 1950-53 Commission.'
(Bob Bolter, November 2001)

John Fairclough, Cheshire, who served on the *Bermuda* from 1957-1959 wrote this article:

'I have just received my copy of the RNA newsletter which refers to HMS *Bermuda's* final commission.

Whilst I didn't serve on her during her final commission, I did serve on her from her commissioning ceremony 26 October 1957 for 14 months, until the completion of my training.

I joined the Royal Navy in October 1956. On completion of my training I was drafted to the *Bermuda* which was completing a two-year refit. We were a general Service Commission and therefore could be sent anywhere. After Christmas leave we set sail for Bermuda and the West Indies. The Captain, R R S Pennyfather, had been based ashore in Bermuda for three years and had promised the people of Bermuda that if he were given command of the ship he would take her there as she had not visited the colony before.

We left the UK as a task force in the company of the RN and Merchant ships and encountered a force nine gale in the mid-Atlantic for several days. As we approached Bermuda we entered the naval harbour at Ireland Island on 30 January 1958. Due to the rough seas we had suffered some damage to equipment on the upper deck and quite a lot of paint had been ripped off the ship's side. Before we could sail into the capital, Hamilton, we had to make good repairs and paint the ship. Once in Hamilton we were dressed overall and open to visitors.

When this visit was over we sailed onto Barbados, Grenada, Dominica, St Lucia, and Bequia. We returned to the UK via a fuelling stop at Punta Delgada in the Azores. After Easter we set sail for Malta to join the Mediterranean Fleet based in Valetta. During our time in Malta we carried out various exercises.

There is a British and Italian grave cemetery in Malta. HMS *Bermuda* and the crew of an Italian cruiser *Duca Delgi Abruzzi* were asked to provide a guard of honour for the wreath laying ceremony. I was a member of that guard of honour.'
(John Fairclough, February 2002)

Stan Bromilow, Scotland, served on the *Bermuda* from 1961-1962.

'I joined *Bermuda* on a cold freezing morning as a "Acting Leading Electrical Mechanic" my first ship after completing the LEM's course in Gosport, Hants. My first sight of the ship was one of dismay. She had just come through what had been one of the worst storms in the North sea in years as a result she was badly damaged. Obviously it didn't take the Dockyard very long to bring her back into shape. She was at this time Flag Ship Home Seas but was getting long in the tooth by now so you can imagine my delight along with many others when it was announced that we were to visit the Island of Bermuda to return the Bell in preparation for the ship to be decommissioned, so it is interesting to hear that the Bell is now in the safe hands of the West Bromwich Branch.

There is a twist or two to this tail, on the way back from the Island of Bermuda where we had been treated like kings the poor old "Bermado" as she was fondly called by all who sailed on her, blew one of her boilers the net result was the crew as a whole were transferred onto HMS *Belfast*.

So you now had a Portsmouth Crew serving on a Plymouth based ship. I don't know how often that happened but it certainly was the topic of conversation with a lot of the old hands at the time.

Bermuda will always have a special place in my heart because I married my better half whilst as a serving member of her ship's crew.'
(Stan Bromilow, January, 2002)

Another e-mail from Stan Bromilow asked to be informed how the *Bermuda* Bell, which he had seen returned to the Island of Bermuda, managed to find its way back to the UK. Bob Bolter, Birmingham Branch of the RNA solved the mystery. He suggested that there were two bells and that the one returned to the people of Bermuda was, in fact, a silver Bell. Stan Bromilow confirmed that it was a silver bell that was left in Bermuda. The original *Bermuda* brass Bell is still in the capable hands of the Trustees of the local branch of the RNA, West Bromwich.

E-mail from Don (Bagsy) Baker, Ex - Engine Room Artificer (ERA)

'Just remembered-very Adrift ERA who wus going OVER the Forth Rail Bridge as Bermuda wus going UNDER it. He caught up with Bermuda at the celebrations after being berthed in our Mess for the Duration – I think he got 30 days stoppage of leave and 30 days stoppage of pay - but then he was a bit of a lad!' *(Don Baker, April 2002)*

The West Bromwich Branch of the Royal Naval Association kindly supplied the following details about West Bromwich and HMS *Bermuda*. The ship was adopted as part of the Warships Week Savings Campaign.

During the whole of the period from about 1942 to 1962 a close liaison was maintained between the ship and the town. For a period at least, Council reports and copies of local newspapers were sent regularly to the ship and full reports of the ship's exploits were sent to Mr Mayor.

First and last Captains respectively were: Captain J S Bethell, Captain M G R Lumby DSO DSC

1947	Ship's Company visited West Bromwich
1956	Lt Commander Brisloe from *Bermuda* attended the dedication of a new Branch Standard for the West Bromwich RNA
1957	Commander M Howard and seven members of the crew came to West Bromwich to open and name "Bermuda Mansions" at the Yew Tree Estate.
1961	Last commissioning at Portsmouth attended by Civic Party.
1965	Council decided that the Bell should be rung at commencement and end of Council Meetings
1965	Trafalgar Day, 21 October, inauguration of ship's Bell took place in the Town Hall.
1976	Metropolitan Borough Council of Sandwell decided to hand over the ship's Bell to the Trustees of the West Bromwich Branch of the RNA.

Jill Taylor (nee Sower), now living in Australia, supplied a copy of a letter from John M Day, Town Clerk, West Bromwich, dated 1 October 1963, which provided a tenuous link with the Town Hall and HM Submarine *Trespasser* which was 'adopted' by the Civil Defence, based in Pitt Street, West Bromwich. This letter stated that the Lord Commissioners at the Admiralty had acceded to the request for a memento from the submarine and had sent along one of the valve wheels, suitably mounted and inscribed. A presentation was made at the Civil Defence Headquarters, Pitt Street. This valve wheel is now in the safe keeping of the Trustees of the local Branch of the Royal Naval Association.

```
COPY OF LETTER RECEVED PROM:
      J.M.DAY, LL.B.
         Town Clerk
            Town Hall, West Bromwich


   H.E.Sower Esq.,
   64 Grafton Road
   WEST BROMWICH.


   Dear Mr. Sower,
                       H.M. Submarine Trespasser

       I have no doubt that you will remember the association
   which existed during the war between the civil defence
   services and H.M. Submarine Trespasser. I understand from Mr.
   Bill Harrison that you were one of the members of the Club
   when it was formed.

       I read some time ago that Trespasser had gone to the
   breakers, and I wrote to the Admiralty asking them if West
   Bromwich could have memento from the ship. You will be very
   interested to learn that the Lords commissioners at the
   Admiralty have acceded to my request for a memento and have
   sent along one of the valve wheels, suitably mounted and
   inscribed. I have suggested to the Civil Defence Committee
   that this ought to find its home at the Civil Defence
   Headquarters and suggested that I should try to get into touch
   with one of the Commanders of Trespasser to see if he could
   come along and make the presentation.

       I have been very thrilled to locate commander Favell, who
   is now living in retirement in Cornwall, and he has indicated
   his willingness to come up to West Bromwich. The Committee
   have agreed that we should arrange a function -and I have been
   asked to do some organising.

       It has now been decided to hold a social evening an
   Thursday, the 16th. October, 1963, at 8.30. p.m. at the Civil
   Defence Social Club, Pitt Street, at which the presentation
   will he made, and the Civil Defence Committee would be very
   pleased if both yourself and Mrs. Sower could come along.

       Prior to this social evening a small dinner party will be
   given at the Pear Tree Club at which a number of official
   guests will be present, and both yourself and Mrs. Sower are
   also cordially invited to join the dinner party, which will
   commence at 7.0. p.m.

       I do hope that it will be possible for you both to be
   present at these functions.

                           Yours sincerely,
                             (Signed)  J.M.DAY.

                                   Town Clerk
```

HM Trespasser "letter" from John M Day, Town Clerk, West Bromwich, to H E Sower, which provides a link with the Town Hall and the submarine which was adopted by the Civil Defence Service, West Bromwich. (Insert) Submarine HM Trespasser at sea. Both images with kind permission of Jill Taylor (nee Sower) Australia.

Crew of HM Trespasser. Kind permission of Jill Taylor, Australia.

HM Trespasser's Mounted Wheel. With kind permission of Royal Naval Association, West Bromwich.

Civil Defence Trespasser Club Programme 1963. With kind permission of Jill Taylor, Australia.

CHAPTER 9

MISCELLANY OF MEMORIES

Contributors: G Welsh; E & I Walker; S Chiles; J M Day; Anon; M Parkes;
J Baggott; M Dallow; H Upton; D Mannering; G Taylor; J Taylor

The main hall has been the venue for many impressive events during the past decades, with some functions obviously more important than others as a landmark in the history of the town. These social occasions are recorded in various ways but they all serve a purpose, in that they describe the major events in the life of the community at both a local and national level. The following memories illustrate the influence this 'magnificent hall' has played in the public and social life of the community during the years.

West Bromwich Weekly News, dated December 1875, in its report on 'Mr Day's Concert in the Town Hall.' provides some insight into the cultural aspirations of the town:

> 'On Monday evening, a concert was given in the Town Hall under the auspices of Mr H Day of the Crystal Palace, Birmingham.
>
> The audience was fairly large, notwithstanding counter attractions. The programme was admirably arranged, passing from grave to gay in the most agreeable manner possible.
>
> But the greatest interest of the audience seemed centred on the second part of the programme which consisted of a variety entertainment.
>
> On the whole the concert was characterised for its refinement and popularity; but we regret to say that during the progress of the entertainment, particularly the first part, that the performers and the respectable section of the audience were repeatedly annoyed by the insane giggling and offensive conduct of a number of roughs in the shilling seats, who imagined that because they had paid their entrance fee they had licence to do as they pleased.
>
> A gentleman belonging to the company remonstrated with the gang, but this had not the slightest beneficial effect. We hope for the sake of the reputation of the town that such unseemly conduct will not be repeated.'

The *West Bromwich Weekly News* 1875 also reported that, on the following Wednesday, a Soiree was held in the Town Hall in the presence of a very small audience. The report continues:

'After the concert, dancing commenced, and at about eleven o'clock there was a considerable influx of visitors. A quadrille band was in attendance, under the leadership of Mr E Dawes. Refreshments were provided by Mr Moore, confectioner. The party did not break up until the small hours of the morning.'

Various sources record public and social events held at West Bromwich Town Hall during the years from 1875 to the present day. These events range from Civic Receptions, 'Grand Concerts' to raise funds for the County Rifle Association, Sunday School Festival Concerts, Soirees, Choral Society Concerts, and an ambitious production of Alberto Randegger's dramatic cantata, *Fridolin* first performed in West Bromwich 1 March 1881, although it was first performed at the *Birmingham Triennial Festival* of 1873.

The following contributors have kindly written about their own experiences, which refer to the part the Town Hall has played in their social lives from the early 1930s to 1973.

Gladys Welsh, a well-known and respected author, kindly supplied this article regarding her memories of a stimulating social life within the Town Hall during the 1930s. Pupils of Guns Village Infants School will remember Gladys Welsh as a teacher during their formative years. Most readers will recognise her name as the author of many articles written in her weekly column for the *Express and Star*.

West Bromwich Town Hall by Gladys Welsh

'In the 1930s West Bromwich Town Hall was a focal point of our lives in many ways. As teenagers we threw ourselves enthusiastically into all kinds of activities. We helped to run bazaars, held in the Town Hall, to raise funds for the building of the new St. Andrew's Church. On the evening of May Day we all went to the pageant of the crowning of the May Queen, when the Town Hall was always full to capacity. Being very young we were bitterly jealous of the May Queen whom we secretly thought was no better looking than we were. We suspected nepotism. The May Queen, the Carnival Queen and the Spirit of the New Year always seemed to be related to the nobs.

The New Year Ball was always well attended. At midnight the dancing stopped and Old Father Time appeared on the stage, long white beard, scythe, et al; followed by the Spirit of the New Year as personified, invariably, by Molly Skidmore. We hated her, too. The fact we ourselves lacked the necessary attributes to be selected as Queens or Spirits of this and that never entered our biased little minds.

Later we regularly went to dances at the Town Hall, some grand, some for charitable causes and some just regular, scum-of-the-mill hops. But, because it was a Town Hall dance we always dressed up to the nines for it, in long chiffon dresses, little velvet boleros or heavily embroidered silk shawls, brocade shoes and masses of Woolworth diamonds on neck, ears, and wrists. I remember one such occasion, just before an election when the Tory candidate, a rather posh gent put in an unexpected appearance accompanied by his 16 year-old daughter. She was dressed in a plain sweater and skirt (probably Cashmere and Jaeger, unknown to us in those days) and made all the rest of us suddenly look like fairies on Christmas trees.

Then there were the free concerts. The Town Hall was open to all, weekends and evenings, for recitals by the Borough Organist (a councillor, acting as MC once famously announced, "Mr Shephard will now play a Fudge by Batch") well known singers and instrumentalists, choirs and operatic groups. There was always something going on at the Town Hall. The days of our youth would have been poorer without the diversions it offered.'

Memories of West Bromwich Town Hall by Edna & Ivan Walker

'Between the years 1935 until the outbreak of war Ballroom Dancing was very popular and the important ones were held in the Town Hall, such as the Mayor's Ball, Christmas and New Years' Eve dances, famous bands were in attendance including Joe Loss and Victor Sylvester.

The Mayor's Ball was always very popular and it was always Evening Dress only, my partner and I always preferred and enjoyed the atmosphere of the New Year's Eve Dance.

On the stroke of midnight the old year (Father Time) was ushered from the stage as the New Year Fairy appeared and everyone cheered the New Year as balloons slowly descended on the dancers. Eventually everyone made their way from the Town Hall in Corporation buses lined up in the adjoining streets ready to take the revellers to various parts of the borough, please note, *no cars* in those days for the majority.

At the above dance on just one occasion whilst dancing I tripped on turning and went down taking my partner with me, it was very embarrassing and she was so annoyed, however she forgave me and later we married. This year we have been fortunate enough to celebrate our Diamond Wedding – happy memories of West Bromwich Town Hall.'

Sam Chiles has fond memories of the dances held in the Town Hall.

Dances in the Town Hall by Sam Chiles

'Dances in the Town Hall were good, nice times. Well, I was President of NALGO, or something like that; Mary Day, the Mayor's Secretary, was on the

Committee. We used to have three or four dances a year in the Town Hall. We hadn't been doing very well with the Annual dance and Mary said,

"I'll tell you what we ought to do, we'll book Victor Silvester."

She was Victor Silvester's cousin so she got him at a reduced price. Now we used to charge about half a crown for a dance in the Town Hall in those days but we put it up to ten shillings for the Baths. I was president of NALGO then and of course we invited the Mayor who wanted to meet Victor Silvester so Mary invited us to the Mayor's Parlour with Victor Silvester so I had to go on stage at the Baths and say a few complimentary things about Victor.

One of the dances was the Toc H in the Town Hall on Easter Tuesday.

Jack Thompson was the leader of Ballroom Dancing in West Bromwich and he used to have the West Bromwich Amateur Ballroom Finals in the Town Hall. One year he invited Santos Cassani, who was the World's Professional Ballroom Champion, to judge the competition and he demonstrated Ballroom Dancing.

There was a sub-way between the front and back offices of the Borough Treasurer's Department. Now in that subway there's a door and it used to lead to outside where coke and coal was stored. Now, if they had any dancing and I didn't want to pay, I used to go and unlock that door, put something against it to stop it rattling, then later that night I would climb over the coal or the coke, push the door open and I was in the building anyway and I'd go to get out in the Borough Treasurer's Department across the corridor and into the dance. Well, that was no trouble.'

Visit to West Bromwich of Max Jaffa and his Orchestra, by John M Day

'I recall meeting Max Jaffa in the Mayor's Parlour at some stage during the evening. Max Jaffa was very popular and for many years appeared for the Season at Scarborough. I remember seeing the Orchestra at Scarborough when Mrs Day was with me at a Conference there. When Ald J J Grant was Mayor (1945-46), he provided cash for four evening concerts with first-rate artists. They were not well supported. West Bromwich was just not ready for music of that kind and he was out of pocket.

However, later on, West Bromwich Education Service provided excellent opportunities for children to learn music. This has been carried forward by Sandwell.

The Town Hall is now regularly used for musical concerts given by the various children's orchestras.'

Another fan of ballroom dancing remembers 'tripping the light fantastic' on the boards at the Town Hall and this account was contributed anonymously.

Big Band Concerts by Anon

'The occasion was the "Big Band Concert" featuring Vic Lewis and his Band. It was a time when music by an American musician named Stan Kenton was popular with quite a few people, and Vic Lewis was his English version and played all Kenton music. The concert was a big success with a full house. Vic ran his band like the Coldstream Guards, they would all sit to attention before Vic made his "Big Entrance", at which point they would stand, Vic tapped his baton once, they all sat, and the concert began. It was fortunate that it was the type of music that did not require a great deal of emotion as none was allowed to be shown by the Band, Vic did not allow it! As the Kenton phase passed, so sadly did Vic and his Band. As far as I can recall there were no further Big Band Concerts at the Town Hall, some said it did not suit the sound. It did not seem suitable as the stage could not be curtained off and performers seemed to have to dash on and off the stage.'

Marie Parkes, of West Bromwich, writes:

'I have a lot of happy memories of West Bromwich Town Hall. As a member of Lyng Girls School we had to sing with other schools. I sat on the stage very near to the organ and we sang *The Ash Grove*.

From St. John's Church we used to hold our "May Festival" at the Town Hall. Many weeks were spent practising. I was so proud in my white dress and white shoes and socks.

There was a May Queen and attendants. One year my elder sister was a Pierrot and a girl named Joan Goodrich was Pierrette. There were stalls all round the hall, selling

West   Bromwich
Trades   and   Labour   Council

★

GRAND   ALL   STAR

VARIETY CONCERT

Town Hall, West Bromwich

Friday, 19th March, 1948

7-30 p.m. prompt

★

PROGRAMME   -   -   -   3d.

Variety Concert Programme, held in the Town Hall 1948, compered by Ray Gibbs, a local man, who produced and compered shows for many different local organisations, including the Old Time Boxers Association. With kind permission of Dr Gerald Gibbs.

homemade goods, sweets, ice cream, tea and cakes. I can still remember the buzzing atmosphere.

One year was the Jubilee of King George and Queen Mary and we all wore red, white and blue ribbons on our dresses. Mrs Jones used to train us and then later Miss Simms "a teacher from Lyng" took over.

Another vivid memory was holding our Speech Day at the Town Hall from West Bromwich Grammar School. We all looked so smart in school uniform and I felt so proud singing in the School Song and the School Hymn. I have been to many carol services, always so well presented.

I helped when the Ebbw Vale Choir visited West Bromwich and all the choir said it had the best acoustics they'd sung at. I was also present when the Canoldir Welsh Choir sang there.

Yes, I've spent many happy hours at the Town Hall and West Bromwich should be proud of it.'

Jean Baggott remembers her school days and voluntary work at the Town Hall:

'In my final year, when I was Head Girl at Spon Lane School, Councillor Medley and his wife were the Mayor and Mayoress. Mrs Medley asked me if I could engage the help of half a dozen girls and organise a series of knitting bees which would held in the Mayor's Parlour. We would be knitting socks for the local hospital and she would be providing the wool and pins. I gave her a helping hand at the occasional 'do' in these hallowed portals, serving tea and biscuits to her guests. One of these events was held in the Council Chamber. I remember the room as being rather grand and highly polished.'

Jean Baggott also recollects some musical entertainment in the Town Hall during her school days which is still popular at the present time and well supported by the Sandwell Youth Music plus families and friends. (*Plate V ii and Plate VII i*)

Choirs, Brass Bands and School Days by Jean Baggott
'I recall a Choral and Brass Band Competition going on there one Saturday. It started at 9 o'clock in the morning and went on till nine o'clock at night. I was there from the word go, taking part with the school choir and I stayed there till the end. At mid-day mother brought some sandwiches and a drink and left my younger brother to spend the day with me. We sat in the balcony looking at the goings on and applauding when necessary. Our school choir had given a concert there a couple of times. We would be crammed into the rooms at the side of the stage and when the audience were seated we would be led out. Mrs Sparks, the choir mistress, (Spon Lane School), thought we were so good that

she arranged for a recording company to bring their equipment to the Town Hall and preserve the sound for all time. We sang, *Where the Bee Sucks* and *All in the April Evening.* We had to make several attempts before it came out right because somewhere in the building someone kept slamming doors.

One function was a display, by all schools, of what was being taught at evening classes in the borough. I'm not sure if evening classes had been available before the war. Mrs Brown, our cookery teacher, had hit on the idea of pinning up a map of England and then running streamers from a particular place to a dish on the table. Eccles cakes were a feature and Brown Windsor soup. There was about two dozen places pinpointed. I was there as the general dogsbody as usual but I always enjoyed these occasions.

I explored every staircase and knew what lay behind every door in the building. Mrs Medley would be heard saying to one of her guests, "Ask Jean. She will know where to find it." And I always did.'

Margaret Dallow is well known for her many interesting articles about local history which are regularly published in *The Black Country Bugle*. The following contribution ranges from reminiscences of social events in the Town hall to an 'historic first' for the youth of the town.

Table Tennis, Swedish Style by Margaret Dallow

'The Town Hall has been the venue for a variety of functions over the years including numerous charity events, concerts and sport. Some of the charity events came in the form of selling goods from stalls, set up in the main hall. Tea and fancy cakes were served in the gallery, from where seated at tables it was possible to view the activity below. One of the most popular stalls was run by my aunt Genny, who sold celluloid cute dolls, which she dressed in crepe paper with matching Juliet caps decorated with sequins.

All Mayoral charity events were popular, especially 'open day' when afternoon teas were given by the newly elected Mayor, whose task it was to meet townspeople he was to serve. Many hands were shaken, and children's heads patted.

West Bromwich can be proud of its many 'firsts'; therefore perhaps one of the most historical event that followed the Second World War was a table-tennis match, for its conception and skilful accomplishment must surely rate a place amongst them.

It was the president, Mr JC Bird and Mr A Wall, the Secretary of the West Bromwich District Table Tennis Association (WBDTTA) who in 1947 invited the Swedish Junior International Team, when on route to the International Games to be held in London in 1948 to visit West Bromwich. Here a match was arranged between the Swedish Juniors - Bengt Nicander, Nils Bergstrom, and Tore Palm - and three young men from the Church Army Club - D Nock, G Markham, and J Round. G Foster from the Camp Street Club was the latter's reserve player. This historic match took place in the Town Hall on the evening of 20 January 1948.

Earlier that day the Swedish team had been greeted in the Mayor's Parlour by the Mayor and Mayoress, Alderman and Mrs G C W Jones, and members of the WBDTTA followed by a meal at the Civic Restaurant, Carter's Green. Shortly before the match the Swedish team met their opponents.

Although the West Bromwich Young men lost, they had played young men who were the best in their country, therefore despite their defeat, they were cheered as heroes by those who had gathered to see a fine example of sportsmanship.

The Swedish Junior International Table Tennis Team, 20 January 1948, played their first match in England against West Bromwich Junior Table Tennis Team. With kind permission of Margaret Dallow.

A final gesture of friendship came from Allan Erikisson, Manager of the Swedish Table Tennis Association who presented Mr Bird with a miniature Swedish flag, hanging from a pole, attached to a base. Later Mr Bird had the base engraved with the names of both teams.'

This letter was sent to Margaret Dallow's father - Mr J C Bird.

Karlstad, May 10th, 1948

Dear Sir,

I have now safely returned from my tour of table-tennis in your beautiful and hospitable country. It was an experience for me to see England and to make you're your acknowledge. When I was at school and read about the great isle on the west I couldn't think, I ever in my life should get a closer acquaintance with it.

All the people I met were friendly and hospitable, and the trip that I have now completed will become a memory in my life. I will heartily thank you for the kindness you have shown me and I fervant hope, that in future, I shall be in a position to see you again.

Yours sincerely,

Tore Palm

This story of a school prize giving concert held in West Bromwich Town Hall by Cronehills School during the 1950s, has winged its way from Australia. It recounts the experiences of two pupils from the school when they were both about fourteen or fifteen years of age.

The Biggest and Most Unlikely by Heather M Upton (nee Patrick)

'My friend Marina Pitt and I were chosen by Miss Stevenson (the school music mistress) to be members of the school choir. One day, I recall Miss Stevenson coming round to our class and listening to the pitch of the voice of each student. Marina and I were only able to hit the low notes, but this is what Miss Stevenson must have been looking for because, to our sheer and utter amazement, we were in! I still wonder, even to this day, just what she saw in Marina and I.

Our appointment was apparently much to the chagrin of many other 'soprano' voiced students – of which we certainly were not! We were far more likely to be considered baritones as much as anything else, if indeed we could be closely associated with any category of pitch at all.

My most vivid memory of Marina and I in the choir was on the occasion of the School Prize Giving at the Town Hall. I remember it as a rather austere, yet grandiose setting for a school event. As members of what was quite a large choir, we occupied the balcony. We faced the stage and had an excellent view of all the teachers in their flowing black gowns, as well as of those students fortunate enough to be in receipt of the prizes. We could only see part of the audience, but I knew that my Nan Evans had walked a considerable distance to be present as the family representative at this special event

As members of the choir we wore the uniform of the Cronehills School. This was a green cotton blouse, a navy tunic as well as white socks with black shoes. In addition to our baritone voices, I guess you could say that at that time Marina and I were both rather generously proportioned. In fact, it could be said that hitting some of the required notes may have placed considerable pressure on the buttons of our tunics at times. At the very least, they certainly didn't do much for our appearance.

The Prize Giving went on for several hours and the choir was required to sing a series of choral pieces throughout. I believe we may have had a piano to accompany us. I still remember Miss Stevenson as being a rather energetic lady who always stood up as she played the piano. Marina and I had no difficulty with singing the low and middle-range notes, but when it came to singing the higher notes, we took the only way out – we mimed! At the time it was almost undoubtedly more important to look good, rather than to sound very, very bad.

After the concert was over, and when we were back at school later that week, a beaming Miss

Boxing Poster – Event held in West Bromwich Town Hall 1949. With kind permission of The Black Country Bugle.

Stevenson came rushing up to us and reported that an elderly lady (whom I knew by the description could be none other than my Nan Evans) had stated that we were, "Better than the Luton Girls' Choir"!

Miss Stevenson may have been very pleased, but for me it was a moment that I truly wanted to die of embarrassment.'

The ex-pupils of Cronehills School appear to have had a traumatic time at the tender age of sixteen, or maybe the fact that that they were in their final year at this establishment affected their judgement, if not their memories. The following memory about a Speech Day at West Bromwich Town Hall was written by Dianne Mannering, (nee Pennington) a well-established free-lance writer of historical books, who has taken time out from writing her new book *A Staffordshire Crown*, to send in this gem of a story. (Some people may recall that in the years of their youth, West Bromwich Town Hall was situated in south Staffordshire, which provided the town with a sense of history). Here Dianne describes a never-to-be forgotten Cronehills Speech Day held in the Town Hall.

Cronehills Speech Day by Dianne Mannering

'The one memory I do have of visiting the Town Hall was when I was sixteen, fresh out of secondary school and confident in my new role as 'an adult'. It was a September evening in 1958 and I went there by invitation to be presented with my school certificate. The Hall was packed with dolled – up parents and the floriferous stage with begonged officials.

I'd left school in July that year to take up a place at Wolverhampton Art College where, joys of all joys, I was required not to wear a uniform.

I'd like to say that I gave my predominately green and ingloriously scruffy uniform to the rag-and-bone man on the day I left Cronehills, but I'm not even sure whether the rag-and-bone man still plied his trade in the Black Lake area by then. I don't really know what became of it, but it was certainly disposed of with undue haste.

In 1958 thick-knit wool hadn't long been on the market and teenage girls were all industriously working away on number 2 needles making cavernous jumpers with intricate cable stitch patterns down the front and called Sloppy Joe's.

So, on the night of the certificate presentations, I turned up at the Town Hall dressed as a 'young adult' in my newly crafted Sloppy Joe, a deep blue corduroy pencil skirt, nylons and square toed, black patent, Louis heeled shoes.

I sniggered when I saw a couple of my contemporaries dressed in school uniform. I was less confident about the situation when a small cluster of my ex classmates arrived, all wearing grey skirts and black blazers. Within ten minutes

I was surrounded by a seething mass of uniformed individuals. It was obvious that everyone except me had taken trouble to read their invitation thoroughly.

It's awful being the odd one out at sixteen!

So my memory of the Town Hall is one of abject mortification as I mounted the stage and walked across to the dignitaries to accept my certificate. I would have given anything to be wearing my despised old school uniform.'

Pop Concerts in the Town Hall by George Taylor

George Taylor recalls various concerts held in the Town Hall, such as pop concerts and other shows including performances by The Bay City Rollers and Tommy Trinder.

'There are still nights when the Town Hall is full of people, for instance, Music Concerts, Remembrance Services and Christmas Carol Services, all of which I have been involved in since 1973 and which continue to date.'

Memories by Jill Taylor

Jill Taylor (nee Sower), lived in West Bromwich until 1954, when she emigrated to Australia. Jill wrote the following account of what part the Town hall had played in her life:

'WANTED: memories of West Bromwich Town Hall – so I read in a letter I received recently and I immediately thought of the three times when the Town Hall marked significant times in my life.

The first time, the year 1945 and I stood amongst a large crowd in the High Street celebrating the end of the war, the lights were on, people were cheering and yet I felt lonely. I wondered where my sailor husband of six months was and what would the future hold for us when he was demobbed. It would mean the end of one part of my life, as I knew he would want to move to his home town of Darwen in Lancashire where a job would be waiting for him. I asked myself how would I manage away from *my* home town?

The year 1954, the second time the Town Hall marked a 'cross road' in my life. It was April and Bob and I with our three small children had decided to immigrate to Australia. We were spending the last few days with my parents and had been invited to a farewell afternoon with the Mayor and Mayoress, Alderman Jack Davies and his wife, and the JP, John Dugdale. A pleasant afternoon was had and as I walked down the steps away from the Town Hall, again I wondered what this move would bring. I was travelling a much further distance from West Bromwich this time, again to an unknown future.

The year 1998, my third 'cross road' and once more I was alone. My husband had died the year previously and I was on my first visit back to West

Bromwich and again I looked at the Town Hall. Forty-four years had gone by since we walked away that afternoon after that visit to the Mayor's Parlour and fifty-three years since I as a nineteen year old had watched the lights come on and wondered what Lancashire would be like, never dreaming that I would one day take a far longer journey from home than the one to Lancashire.

I may never see my home town again but I shall always remember the Town Hall just for those three times when it marked the most important choices in my life.' (*Plate VI i*)

CHAPTER 10
DRAMA BEHIND THE SCENES

After the trauma and shortages of the War years, some attempt was made to bring a little pleasure into the social life of the inhabitants of the Town. The Town Hall played its part by once more being the venue for varied leisure pursuits which involved a lot of effort and extra work for the Corporation and its workforce. As Reg Thompson recalled:

'Life at the Town Hall hasn't always been quiet I can tell you that. An order came through to replace the Baths Floor and the Deputy Surveyor - a smashing bloke he was - came down to see us and said, "I want you to go round to the Baths and sort a portion of the flooring out and put it down in the hall. They're having a new floor in the Baths and we're having what we want of the old one in the hall." It's still down now, a Maple floor.'

It was an amateur dramatic production, staged in the main hall, which caused the most angst and stress for everyone, when it was decided in 1948 to produce a play in the Town Hall about the Tudor House situated in the town.

Drama in the Hall - The Oak House Pageant
It may seem strange to include the Oak House in a history of the Town Hall when, at first sight, the only thing they have in common is the great benefactor, Reuben Farley. As Mayor of the town he presented the Oak House as a museum to the inhabitants of West Bromwich.

As elaborate plans were made for a play about the Oak House to be staged in the Town Hall, behind the scenes, other equally dramatic scenarios were gradually unfolding. John M Day supplied the background information to this ambitious production about the history of Oak House, West Bromwich. He recalled:

'Reuben Farley acquired the Oak House and presented it to the Council in 1899. Later, the house was used as a Museum. It contained a miscellany of exhibits. There were birds' eggs, stuffed animals and the like. When I first saw the Oak House, the Curator was a Mrs Parry. Her husband was, for a time, a Member of the Council.

After the war, a suggestion was made that the House should revert back to its original use as a Yeoman's House. To this end, the exhibits were removed and the house was re-furbished. The House needed some refurbishing with period furniture; we sought help from a specialist firm in London. They acquired suitable examples, which were purchased. New curtains were required and specially made in period style. The firm from London negotiated the loan of several items from the Victoria and Albert Museum. When the refurbishment was completed, the house looked really grand.

Ald G E Powell was Chairman of the Committee responsible for the House and the idea of commemorating the 50th Anniversary of the gift to the Council was drafted. The house had a long history of having been built in Tudor times and a good deal of information about it was available. I am not sure just where the idea for a play about the House came from; but it was decided to purchase it.

At the time, there were several Amateur Groups interested in drama and they were invited to become involved. The first thing was to find an author to prepare a script. At the time, the BBC had used a Mr L du Garde Peach on several programmes. He was approached to see whether he would tackle the job and he agreed. I do not recall his fee for the job.

The play consisted of several Cameos depicting various highlights of events. The local groups undertook to be responsible for acting these Cameos. A professional Producer, Heath Joyce, an eminent London producer was engaged and rehearsals began. *(ref: Midland Chronicle 1948)*

There was a great deal to be done. The Town Hall needed space to create a stage; scenery was hired; stage lighting etc; had to be put in. Costumes were ordered from a firm in London. Town Hall seating had to be set up and the rows and chairs numbered.

Sale of the tickets was entrusted to my Department and involved a great attention to detail. Nothing like this had been attempted previously. The show ran for two weeks, I think. The sale of tickets did not cover the outlay, but the play was well received and enjoyed by many.

The time arrived for the dress rehearsal, but the costumes had not arrived by the weekend before final rehearsals were due.

On the Saturday morning, I took on the job of trying to locate them. They were coming from London by train. Enquiries at West Bromwich Station drew a blank. I borrowed a car plus Corporation driver and we went first to New Street Station – no joy! A clerk in the parcel department advised we try Moor Street. The baskets were not in the parcels department there either! But, all was not lost; I was told that a goods train was parked in the sidings, but had yet not been emptied, so, guided by the parcels employees, we walked along the rails and there in one of the wagons was what I was looking for. So, the problem was overcome at, virtually, the eleventh hour!

It may not be generally known, but every new script for public showing needs the prior approval of the Lord Chamberlain. This was another job, which I dealt with.

History tells us that the noted Methodist Preacher, John Wesley, visited Oak House and preached in front of the building during a snowstorm. This event formed one of the Cameos. The producer needed snow! He advised that this could be overcome by using cinematography. The necessary equipment was hired, and the resulting snow effect was very, very good.'

While the calamity of the missing costumes was being sorted out by John Day, the local work-force was being deployed to avert another possible disaster by trying to trace the whereabouts of some missing stage curtains.

Reg Thompson takes up the story:

'We had the Oak House Pageant in the Town Hall. For the first three or four days there was nobody there. Well, if it hadn't been for us there wouldn't have been anybody at all.

At that time I was working at Hill & Long's and I was at work that Saturday morning. When I came out my brother was sitting there on his bike and he said, "Come and give us a lift at the Town Hall"

So we went to the Town Hall and there was the scaffolding but no curtains.

They (the hire firm) phoned up at 11.30 am and said we couldn't have them. They'd sent them somewhere else so we've got no curtains. You can imagine the height of them.

I suggest that if we get the consent of Mr Dallow, who was the Deputy Surveyor, to go round to the Baths, steal the curtains and rails off the three big windows and use these curtains.

The Superintendent of the Baths walked in and said, 'What's going on?' We explained, so we had the rails and the curtains and I came home and fetched the sewing machine. Six of us went into the Committee Room A and we measured the curtains out and we were about six feet short in the drop and we could have done with another 6ft. wide. So we got a roll of blackout curtain and we started sewing and finished at two o'clock on the Sunday morning. We made the curtains and we made the curtains work. It was a theatrical firm from Manchester who let us down.

The first two nights were dead, then people started to get to know about it and in the end we couldn't get them all in. It was absolutely choc-a-bloc. It was really a marvellous show they put on. It was a pity it ended.'

The stories previously related reveal the amount of work and dedication required to make a success of an ambitious project. The latest techniques of cinematography used to obtain the special effects of falling snow, recalls another snow- scene recreated within this magnificent hall, nearly half a century earlier. On that occasion however, in 1904, a "well-known Bazaar Artist" was employed to create, not one building, but a whole Alpine Village.

The senses reel under the magnitude of the task to recreate an alpine scene within the restrictions of the main hall. One can imagine the good-natured banter between the various stallholders, the smell of the various delicacies and the noise level magnified and echoing through the hall.

The Alpine Village Bazaar, 1904

This Grand Alpine Village Bazaar was in aid of the Ebenezer New School Building Fund to raise £500. It was held in West Bromwich Town Hall on November 22, 23 & 24, 1904. Although the condition of the original *Official Handbook*, by Clift Bros., Printers, West Bromwich, is in a poor condition, it is, nevertheless, an impressive record of that event.

Scenic description is as follows:

'The visitor on entering the Hall will find himself apparently in the very heart of an Alpine Village, quietly reposing beneath the eternal Alps – the rugged peaks covered with perpetual snow – towering away into the distance.

On either side are the Chalets, the lower portions being converted into shops, at which will be found an abundant supply of all kinds of articles, useful and ornamental. Here, ready cash can be rapidly converted into substantial goods.

One end of the village is bounded by rushing mountain torrents, behind which is a stretch of Alpine scenery, beautifully painted and giving a view of

Ebenezer Congregational Church Bazaar Programme, 1904. With kind permission of Pauline Hale.

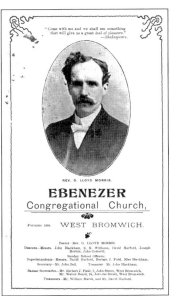

(left) Bazaar Programme, 'Olympic Marionettes', 1904. With kind permission of Pauline Hale. (middle) Bazaar programme 'West Bromwich Pierrots', 1904. With kind permission of Pauline Hale. (right) Ebenezer Congregational Church Pastor – Rev O Lloyd Morris, 1904. With kind permission of Pauline Hale.

the tops of the distant mountains in a most realistic manner. Facing this, and as it were, holding guard over the whole scene, stands a grand old turreted Castle, which displays the characteristic architecture of the country.

The whole effect of the scenery is heightened by the brightening influence of a snowstorm, which has apparently just passed over, and its frozen crystals, gleaming in the light, sparkle like a thousand diamonds.'

In contrast, the cold Alpine scene at the turn of the century was replaced with visions of a hall filled with the sight and perfume of countless flowers as recalled in the following reminiscences by Anon:

The Hall in Bloom - The Chrysanthemum Society by Anon

There was a time, many moons ago, when the Town Hall stage would be a blaze of colour and the hall would be filled with the heavy perfume of the flowers provided by the Borough's Parks Department but, alas, those heady days have long since gone. However, this does not prevent the scene being recaptured and kept alive by the vivid memories of this anonymous contributor and others who were members of the Chrysanthemum Society:

'My last contact with the Town Hall was in the middle fifties. My father had taken a great interest in growing Chrysanths just after the war and had joined the West Bromwich Chrysanthemum Society. It was well supported in the early days but lost some support and relied on a hard core of workers to keep it going. He remained with it for forty years.

The Society held two Shows each year, the Early, in September and the Late, in November. They were held in the Main Hall of the Town Hall. It was about that time that the Society could not find a Secretary and I offered to help until someone could be found. One of the first jobs was to write to the then current Mayor of West Bromwich asking for his indulgence in allowing the Society the FREE use of the Town Hall for two occasions, the free bit was important because the Society was short on funds. Each year the Mayor would graciously grant the Society two dates for its Shows. This went on for many years, probably until the late sixties and early seventies.

On the Friday night before the Show, the Hall had to be prepared, tables laid out and covered in black cloth (left over from the blackout?) the green vases all placed in position and all the prize cards to be written out and the Cups and Medals polished ready to be put on show. The Friday before the Show was a hive of activity as exhibitors prepared their blooms with tender loving care, curling the petals to shape with tweezers and brushing the flowers with the softest of brushes. There was always plenty of jostling for position on the tables for the exhibits and differences could get heated at times.

One of the main players in all this was the Caretaker who was usually around to sort out odd problems. He seemed to live in the Town Hall, being contacted by a side door in Lodge Road. The other request we made to His Worship, was to Open the Show, which he did on many occasions, after all the growers were also voters!

The big day started early with the exhibitors still preparing their blooms up to the moment when the Judges arrived and began their task of picking the winners of the various classes. The Hall was a pretty sight to see, with all the various blooms on show from far and wide. People came many miles to show their blooms at West Bromwich Town Hall on Show Day.

The Mayor and his entourage would arrive after judging was completed and the public was allowed in. It was never a "packed house" but quite a few people came along to see the Show. When the Show closed the blooms not taken away by their owners were auctioned off for the benefit of the Society's funds by a well known West Bromwich estate auctioneer. It always seemed sad that such wonderful blooms were sold off, and latterly given away, for such a small amount.

In later years the West Bromwich Chrysanthemum Society moved from its home in the Town Hall, to various other venues, but it was never quite the same show that went on in the Town Hall.' (*Plate VI ii*)

Ratcliffs Party by Reg Thompson

Ratcliffs Party provides us with an insight into the generosity of some of the firms who wished to support the local community. Reg recalled:

'Ratcliffs used to put a party on every year, from Great Bridge Tools. They would decorate the hall and all the rest of it. I was very friendly with Mary Day, the Mayor's Secretary, and she sent for me one day and asked me to help with a party for the physically handicapped people.

Well, I hadn't announced it but at the time we were running the Social Club at the Public Works. I only asked for help and we had fourteen volunteers immediately. Well, we did it the first year and when the show was over, I said to Mary, "There's only one thing wrong here. Wouldn't they like a drink of beer? Find out for the next time." So she found out and I got on to Ansells and said, "We're having a function at the Town Hall for the handicapped people and we want a couple of barrels of beer, how about it?" And the chap said, "Alright. We'll supply you and with the glasses."

They came and set it all up and you've never seen anything like it! They were drinking a pint of beer whether they wanted a pint or not. And then, Ratcliffs always put a huge net in the roof with balloons in and they were asked not to let them down as it was for us to do that. Well, we let them down and there were people in the wheelchairs jumping up to and catching the balloons. I've never seen anything like it! Nobody hurt themselves and I remember one chap had got six. God knows why he wanted six!

We had another party there for children. It started off at Cronehills when there was 299 so we decided to have it in the Town Hall. Now, to get the Town Hall, the Committee could give you the Town Hall for free. If you wanted the heating on the Mayor would do that - he would give you permission for the heating because this is the way it worked. Well, we got the lot so we had this party for 380 and when we'd finished there must have been 6,000 because they'd come in from everywhere.

We'd got stacks and stacks of presents. I said to one chappie named Charlie, who was very much a family man, "I've got a job for you. I want you to be Father Christmas."

So, we go to the Baths and borrowed the sleigh we'd built for letting in the New Year, took it to the Town Hall and when the time came we put a rope down on the floor, got the sleigh outside behind the front door, sat Charlie in and slowly pulled it in. Oh, the children absolutely loved it! He gets out of the sleigh, goes and sits on the stage and we'd got children from two years up to fifteen. The first one went up and he said, "That aye Father Christmas that's Charlie." He was only a tiny tot and Charlie said, "That's it ! I've had it," and he had to come off.

The laugh was, when we took him out, the kids pushed him in the sleigh and if it hadn't been for the fact that the doors were shut he would have been across the road. They pushed him so fast and slammed on the door that it started to rattle. But that's the only party we had of that size!'

The Albion and the Cup by Reg Thompson

'When the Albion won the Cup we decided to decorate the hall. Well, we put blue and white crepe paper all round the gallery. I sewed it all at home, hours and hours on the machine. Then we got a blue and white flag that we draped all round the pole. I made twelve rosettes to pin on the base and we made two or three very big ones which we made for the hall to put in front of the stage. We put a table in front of it all and decorated it blue and white.

Then we used to have a workshop under the stage and a policeman came down and said, "Look after this box will you?"

I said, "Why what's the matter with it?"

He said, "The Cup's in there. Will you look after it while I go home to my lunch."

But he said, "When you open it you will be surprised because the colour of it is yellow."

Two of us worked well over an hour to clean it. We used a tin of Silvo. We cleaned it up, it was shining. We put it back in the box and it was put in position.

There were people invited to that function who probably didn't know where the Albion ground was. We were invited and the two chauffeurs and six others of us were invited to have the same meal but we had to go into a room at the back of the stage. It was probably one of the best meals I've ever had in my life.

But the thing that made me smile was when I asked how much we'd got to spend on decorations, it was only £24. We had to do everything for £24. We pinched this and pinched that. The people who helped us out more than anybody were the electric people who had the Electric Department at the top of Church Lane, where the *Express and Star* is. They used to generate their own electricity in West Bromwich and they sent the fellas and the foreman said, "Whatever you want, just say, and we'll do it."

And they helped us and they paid for it because we could still only spend £24. The crepe paper cost more than that! We were all putting our hands in our own pockets to help out the cost and hours and hours of time. We overcame all that and it was all a great success to me.'

CHAPTER 11

GUARDIANS OF THE TOWN HALL

The Town Hall Keepers of each age have faithfully kept watch over the fabric of the hall and the well-being of those who enter the building. The term Keeper of the Hall, as distinct from the modern title of Curator, conjures up more of a sense of history and pride in the building, including its heritage, rather than the title of a person who has acquired some specialised knowledge.

There have been many Hall Keepers who have taken pride in their work within the building and over the years have won the respect of their colleagues and members of the public. Unfortunately, to date, there appears to be no record of their names or terms of office, therefore the following information is of great interest.

Frances G Walton, who lives in Aldridge, kindly forwarded this interesting information about the first "Keeper of the Town Hall" which she discovered while researching her family history last year.

Richard Moore
Curator (Keeper) of West Bromwich Town Hall
from 1875-1898
'Richard was the son of Joseph Moore and lived in the Greets Green area of West Bromwich. In 1863 he married my Great, Great, Great Aunt, Ellen Moreton – at the time of his marriage his occupation was a furnaceman.
In 1875 he became "Keeper" of the Town Hall and he and Ellen resided there until his death in 1898. He was buried in Heath Lane Cemetery just inside the Heath Lane entrance amongst other Council Officers. The Headstone Inscription reads:

In Loving memory of
Richard Moore
for 23 years the Keeper
Of the Town Hall, West Bromwich
Who died Sept. 30th 1898
Aged 56 yrs.
Thy Will be Done

Frances Walton also supplied the following extract from a local newspaper, dated 30.9.1898.

'DEATH OF THE WEST BROMWICH TOWN HALL KEEPER
We regret to announce the death of Mr. Richard Moore, aged 56, which took place this morning. Deceased was hall keeper at the Town Hall, West Bromwich, which office he had held for over twenty years. He was a faithful public servant, always of a genial disposition, and was greatly respected. Mr. Moore had been ailing for some time.'

It is a fascinating fact that Richard Moore and his wife Ellen, who also became the Town Hall Keeper following her husband's death, would have known many of the people mentioned in the early research regarding the history of the Town Hall and they would have worked in the building as it is described in this report from the 1875 *West Bromwich Weekly News*:

'Noticing the Town Hall it must at the outset be admitted that the place is one which in every sense of the word is a credit to the town. It is an architectural triumph of which the people of West Bromwich need justly be proud. It is

The Civic Regalia of the boroughs of Wednesbury and Tipton went on display in West Bromwich Town Hall in 1972. Sam Copson, curator and Sargeant at Arms for the Mayor of West Bromwich is seen here looking at the Tipton collection. (With kind permission of Sam Copson's family). (Photo: With kind permission of the Express and Star).

commodious, and admirably adapted for all public wants whether they embrace the exciting, political question of the hour that have to be ventilated, or whether an entertainment of a lighter kind is needed in the shape of an evenings theatrical or vocal amusement.'

It is impossible in this selection of memories, which span such a short time in the life of the Town Hall, to evaluate whether it has lived up to the expectations of our predecessors.

In the early years of its construction, the Town Hall appears to have fulfilled its role to provide a nucleus for the newly emerged borough's political and social requirements. The passing of time has seen a decline in its use as a venue for the social life of the town's inhabitants and the elements have been rather unkind to the condition of the fabric of the building.

During the ensuing years some attempt was made to periodically update the Town Hall's image, most spectacularly in 1969, when the Mayor appealed in Committee and in the local newspapers for a brighter town. He boldly declared that, "The exterior of the building will be steam cleaned, woodwork repainted and notice-boards redesigned."

After a heated debate during a committee meeting those members in favour of the resolution won the day. Thus, to the consternation of the more faint-hearted members of the council, the building was given "a make-over" in the form of a steam- clean, with the walls valiantly surviving this onslaught to their pride and dignity, despite predictions to the contrary and visions of a mass of crumbling stone-work.

It is a sad reflection upon the standards of today's society that the entrance to the Town Hall is gained, not through the grand hallowed steps of the main entrance in High Street, but via the rear of the building where staff and visitors alike gain access through automatic doors, and an array of coded security locks before arriving at their final destination.

Great technological advances have been made in the world since the construction of this Grade II Listed Building and society has moved on since that era but due, perhaps, to a lack of investment in the building and the transfer of power to the Council Offices in Oldbury, the Town Hall has ceased to play a major role within the town. It lacks that sense of vibrancy and atmosphere common to the building during its early years when it fully represented the civic and secular needs and interests of the general public.

It would be difficult to disagree with the opinions of the older generation of West Bromwich, who treasure happy memories of a stimulating social life provided by the Town Hall of their youth, that it is a great loss to the town that the building has not retained a central role within the life of the community.

It seems an opportune moment to recall that the Town Hall was built when the town obtained its important Charter of Incorporation with its Grant of Arms in 1882 during the reign of one Queen, (Victoria) and that, coinciding with this year, 2002, our present Queen (Elizabeth II) is celebrating her Golden Jubilee year in many ways including the lottery funding of the Queen's Award. One of these, '*Awards for All,*' has so generously been granted to West Bromwich Library User Group to fund the research, and publish this book on West Bromwich Town Hall, for which all of those involved in the project are very grateful.

On a more positive and optimistic note, the Town Hall may, in future years, regain its status due to the proposed regeneration of West Bromwich Town Centre, which will provide it with a new role so that eventually it may find a place in the affections and fond memories of future generations.

Anne Wilkins, August 2002

APPENDIX 1

THE CHARTER OF INCORPORATION

The West Bromwich Town Improvement Commissioners

Minute Book 5 (Accounts Book) Feb 1882 – July 1884
The First meeting of the Town Council, Thursday 9 Nov 1882.
At this historic meeting the Charter of Incorporation was entered into the Minutes.
  The following extract is a section of 'The Charter' taken from the official records.

THE CHARTER OF INCORPORATION

Mr Alfred Caddick read the Charter of Incorporation at a Council meeting.
It was moved by J Arthur Kenrick Esq., seconded by Mr Councillor Farley
and it was resolved:
That the Charter be entered on the minutes

Victoria, by the Grace of God,
of the United Kingdom of Great Britain and Ireland Queen
Defender of the Faith

To all to whom these present shall come, greeting, *Whereas,* by the Municipal
Corporations (New Charters) Act 1877 it was enacted that if on petition to Her
majesty of the Inhabitant Householders of any Town or towns, or District in
England or of any of those inhabitants, praying for the grant of a Charter of
Incorporation Her Majesty by the advice of Her privy Council should think fit by
Charter to create such Town or Towns or District or any part thereof specified in
the Charter, with or without any adjoining place a Municipal Borough and to
Incorporate the Inhabitants thereof, it should be lawful for Her Majesty by the
Charter to extend to that Municipal Borough and the Inhabitants thereof so
incorporated the provisions of the municipal Corporation Act.

And Whereas by the said Municipal Corporations (New Charters) Act 1877 it
was further enacted that every petition for a Charter under that Act should be
referred to a Committee of the Lords of Her Majesty's Privy Council (in that Act
referred to as the Committee of Council) and that one month at least before the
petition should be taken into consideration by the Committee of Council notice
thereof and of the time when the same would be taken into consideration by the

Committee of Council should be published in the London Gazette and otherwise in such manner as might be directed by the Committee of Council for the purpose of making it known to all persons of interest.

And Whereas certain Inhabited Householders of the Parish of West Bromwich in the County of Stafford have petitioned *US* for the grant of a Charter of Incorporation

And Whereas such petition was referred to a Committee of *Our* Privy Council and one month at least before the same was taken into consideration by the said Committee notice thereof and of the time when the same was so to be taken into consideration was duly published in the London gazette and otherwise as directed by the Committee.

And Whereas our Privy Council have recommended *US* to grant this Charter of Incorporation. We therefore as well as by virtue of *OUR* Royal perogative as of the powers given to *US* by the Municipal Corporations (New Charters) Act 1877 or any other Act and of all other powers and authorities enabling *US* by this advice of our Privy Council do hereby grant and declare as follow.

1. The Inhabitants of the Parish of West Bromwich in the County of Stafford within the limits set forth in the first schedule to these present and their successors shall be one body politic and corporate by the name of the Mayor, Aldermen and Burgesses of the Borough of West Bromwich with perpetual succession and a common seal, and may assume armorial bearings (which shall be duly enrolled in the Herald's College) and may take and hold such lands and hereditainents within the Borough as may be necessary for the site of buildings and premises required for the official purposes of the Corporation and other the purposes of the said Municipal Corporation Acts.

2. The Mayor, Aldermen and Burgesses of the said Borough shall have the powers, authorities, immunities and privileges usually vested by law in the Mayor, Aldermen and Burgesses of a Municipal Borough and the provisions of the said Municipal corporations Acts shall extend to the said Borough and the Inhabitants thereof Incorporated by this Charter;

3. The number of Councillors of the Borough shall be eighteen;

4. The Borough shall be divided into six wards with the names and bounds specified in the first schedule of these present;

5. Each of the said Wards shall elect three Councillors;

6. For the purposes of making the said Municipal Corporation Acts applicable in the case of the first constitution of the Borough *WE* do hereby so far as regards the first Burgess List, Burgess Roll and election of Councillors, mayor, Aldermen, Auditors, Assessors, Town Clerk and Treasurer of the Borough fix and order as follows:

(a) The days and times mentioned in the second column of the first part of the Second Schedule to those presents (in lieu of the days set opposite thereto in the first column of the same part of the same Schedule) shall be the days and times on, at or before which the various acts and things in relation to the matters aforesaid are to be done and the said days and times mentioned in the said second column shall be respectively substituted in the Municipal Corporation Acts for the days and times set opposite thereto in the said column, and

(b) The Town Hall, High street shall be the place at which any list, notice or document required to be affixed on or near the outer door of the Town Hall....

In Witness whereof we have caused these our letters be made patent
Witness ourself at our own Palace at Westminster the thirteenth day of
September in the forty sixth year of our reign
By Her Majesty's Command

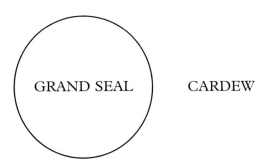

GRAND SEAL   CARDEW

BIBLIOGRAPHY

Birmingham Artists Vol.1, Pt.2: 1875-1880 (compilation in Birmingham Reference Library)
Birmingham Biography 1881-1886 (collection of newspaper cuttings in Birmingham Reference Library)
Briggs, Geoffrey *Civic and Corporate Heraldry* Heraldry Today 1971
Chance Brothers & Co. *Mirror for Chance* (produced for the Festival of Britain 1951)
Ebenezer Congregational Church Official Bazaar Handbook Clift Bros., West Bromwich
Geometrical and Roman Mosaics, Encaustic tile Pavements and Enamelled Wall Decorations by Wyatt M. Digby, etc. (publication in Ironbridge Gorge Museum)
Hackwood, Frederick W. *A History of West Bromwich* "Birmingham News" 1895
A History of West Browich by G. C. Baugh, M.W. Greenslade, and D.A. Johnson (being an extract from *The Victoria History of the County of Stafford* Vol. XVII, originally published 1976 for the University of London Institute of Historical Research) Staffordshire County Council 1987
Maw & Co. Catalogue
Pine, L.G. *Dictionary of Mottoes* Routledge & Kegan Paul 1983
Sandwell Metropolitan Borough Council (Legal Department) *Deeds of Conveyance* for William Izon deceased
Webster, James Carson *The Labors of the Months, In Antique & Mediaeval Art to the End of the Twelfth Century* Northwestern University, Evanston and Chicago, USA 1938
West Bromwich Town Improvement Commissioners *Improvement Commissioners Minutes Book 2: 25 Nov 1863 - 4 Dec 1872*
Book 5 (Accounts): Feb 1882 - July 1884
West Bromwich Trade Directory Vol. 3 1870-1884 (compilation in Sandwell Community History and Archives Service)

Birmingham Morning News 9 August 1874
The Building News 27 October 1871
Daily Gazette 1875
The Free Press 9 December 1882
Midland Chronicle May 1978
West Bromwich Weekly News 14 Aug 1875